I0605792

Lewis Carroll
Collections & Collectors

Lewis Carroll Collections & Collectors

EDWARD GUILIANO

PUBLISHED BY THE

LEWIS CARROLL SOCIETY OF NORTH AMERICA

& DISTRIBUTED BY THE

UNIVERSITY OF VIRGINIA PRESS

CHARLOTTESVILLE & LONDON

Contents

UP THE RABBIT-HOLE

PRELIMINARY THOUGHTS ON CARROLL COLLECTIONS & COLLECTORS

Humans collecting objects appears to be primordial – or at least the practice is ancient and is evident in many diverse societies. Collecting manuscripts and books goes back as far as the existence of texts and books that could be collected. One proof point in the ancient world is the famous Library of Alexandria, founded in the third century B.C.E., which at some stage may have included as many as half a million papyrus scrolls. It was certainly the largest collection of manuscripts in the ancient world, and featured works by Plato and Aristotle, the way rare book and research libraries today possess the works of Shakespeare or Dickens or, in many instances, the works of Lewis Carroll. Imagine that. It is unlikely that Charles Lutwidge Dodgson (hereafter mostly referred to by his popular pen name, Lewis Carroll) ever did.

But Carroll would fully appreciate the appeal of collecting. He was a collector himself. It is not clear that anyone fully understands the complex appeal of collecting, especially the individual psychological motivations, yet it is clear that a collection or being a collector involves active engagement, intention, and focus. Books on a shelf, or two or three, or clothes stuffed into closet after closet, do not make a book collection or a wardrobe or fashion collection. Accumulations are not collections. Collecting evokes memories, happiness, and serves emotional well-being; but thoughts are collateral aspects of collecting and do not, strictly speaking, constitute a collection. Only tangible things do. The notion of order or ordering is also a key characteristic of a collection or collector.

Carroll "tirelessly collected gadgets, toys, games, puzzles, and mechanical and technological inventions," Carroll's biographer, Morton Cohen, noted. He liked to amuse himself, and also entertain his family and friends. He liked pseudo magical tricks and was adept at performing some. Carrollians – which includes Lewis Carroll scholars, fans, and collectors – know about

Bob the Bat, his mechanical bird that flew around powered by an elastic band. They know about his music boxes, his orguinette, his electric pen, his early typewriter.

What does one make of his more than two hundred fountain pens if they are not a collection? Unless it was simply an accumulation. Doubtful – though Carroll could be compulsive. He certainly was a compulsive indexer. As many readers will recall, this is a man who for the last thirty-seven years of his life famously kept a register of all the letters he wrote or received and cross-indexed them for content. The register contained 98,721 items. For four decades, he kept an account of dinner parties he attended, including a seating chart and menus. He certainly found sanity in the ordering of things. In his life and in his writings, he strove to achieve pure order.

In his everyday life and in his fiction and nonfiction writing, his quest for order was not singular. As Carroll expert Donald Rackin has observed, "People like Dodgson, people who manifest their extraordinary need for order by obsessively regulating their everyday lives, seem also to manifest through this behavior a deep-seated anxiety about the messiness that surrounds us, an anxiety about the morally random nature of existence. On guard against this apparently mindless-less chaos that threatens their beliefs and their very sanity, they fill their waking lives with artificial structure – with manufactured systems and rules their wills impose on all the disorderly matter and events they inevitably encounter."

Not in extremis, but collecting as a self-defense and exercise in good mental health practices, is a factor that can explain its ubiquitous practice. It is good for you. And in Carroll's case, we have the benefit of him also working out his anxieties about death and dying, society and structure, love and loss, in the *Alice* books.

Carroll notably collected photographs – his, but also those of contemporaries whom he admired – and kept them in photo albums. He also owned some contemporary

Carroll's photograph of his Christ Church study

art. Carroll's personal library of books has been estimated to number about three thousand. While he did not "collect" books, the size and breadth of his library reflects his curious mind. And the runs of books, for example, on women, on medicine, and other specialized topics were studiously acquired. Still, his unusually large personal library was mostly for reading.

But he did have collection exceptions. He had a full set of Charles Dickens's works, for example. And as Jeffrey Stern has noted in his study of Carroll's library, he secured facsimile reproduction copies of several authors' works, including Dickens's *A Christmas Carol*, a reprint of the first edition of Daniel Defoe's *Robinson Crusoe*, a facsimile of the first edition of John Milton's *Paradise Lost,* as well as three rare John Keats first editions. "The preponderance of facsimile printings might suggest that Carroll agrees with the sensible notion, prevalent among collectors," according to Stern, "that the original appearance of a text was an important aid in understanding its full meaning." That certainly aligns with Carroll's meticulous care of how his own publications looked and were produced.

While Carroll's tastes could be eclectic, his collecting impulses were akin to those of many educated Victorians. They passionately and avidly collected a wide range of objects, such as art and antiquities, insects and butterflies, seashells and marine specimens, plants and botanical specimens, coins and stamps, postcards and trade cards, minerals and fossils, jewelry, stuffed animals and birds, maps and globes, photographs, including fan memorabilia, and, of course, books and manuscripts. By the end of the Victorian era, people were collecting Lewis Carroll.

Posthumous painting of Carroll (1899) from photographs by Hubert von Herkomer, now hanging at Christ Church, Oxford

Begin at the Beginning of Carroll Collections

Though Carroll's friends and family retained various copies of Carroll's books, photographs, and letters that he sent or gave them during his lifetime, that is more a passive action than active collecting. Many of his child friends and their parents kept his gifts, perhaps out of fondness for the man and their memories of him, but perhaps also because he had gained celebrity status as the author of the *Alice* books. Certainly, copies of photographs he took found their way into many Victorian albums compiled by families who knew him. But the practice, now in its second century, of actively collecting "things Carroll" can be traced to the sale of his effects upon his death.

When Carroll died on January 14, 1898, at age sixty-five, his passing was an international event. Obituaries around the world marked his unique imagination and his place among great artists and authors. His college rooms at Christ Church, Oxford, were required quickly for their next don, and his possessions needed to be distributed or destroyed. His brother Wilfred thought it best not to have all his papers carted to the family home, but to have many

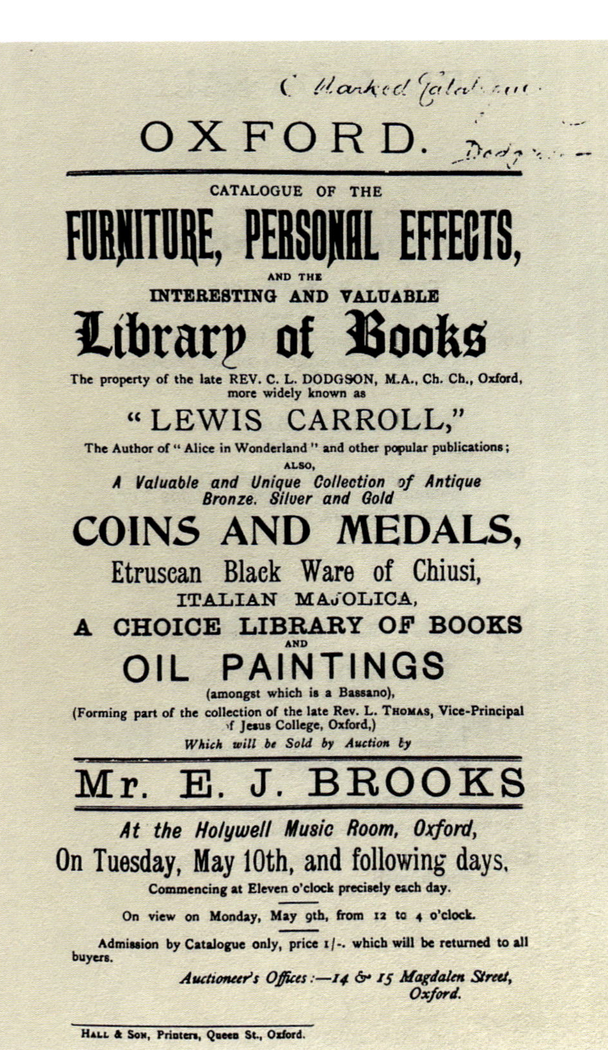

OXFORD.

CATALOGUE OF THE

FURNITURE, PERSONAL EFFECTS,

AND THE

INTERESTING AND VALUABLE

Library of Books

The property of the late REV. C. L. DODGSON, M.A., Ch. Ch., Oxford, more widely known as

"LEWIS CARROLL,"

The Author of "Alice in Wonderland" and other popular publications;

ALSO,

A Valuable and Unique Collection of Antique Bronze, Silver and Gold

COINS AND MEDALS,

Etruscan Black Ware of Chiusi,

ITALIAN MAJOLICA,

A CHOICE LIBRARY OF BOOKS

AND

OIL PAINTINGS

(amongst which is a Bassano),

(Forming part of the collection of the late Rev. L. Thomas, Vice-Principal of Jesus College, Oxford,)

Which will be Sold by Auction by

Mr. E. J. BROOKS

At the Holywell Music Room, Oxford,

On Tuesday, May 10th, and following days,

Commencing at Eleven o'clock precisely each day.

On view on Monday, May 9th, from 12 to 4 o'clock.

Admission by Catalogue only, price 1/-. which will be returned to all buyers.

Auctioneer's Offices:—14 & 15 Magdalen Street, Oxford.

Hall & Son, Printers, Queen St., Oxford.

Cover page of the Brooks 1898 auction catalog following Carroll's death

burned or dispersed in Oxford. And so it came to pass. The family retained some of his papers and other possessions, but all those books and furnishings from his rooms, his nyctograph, photographs, games, and gadgets? In the world of Carroll collectors, it is well known they were disposed at a two-day auction of his furniture, personal effects, and library in Oxford on May 10 and 11, 1898, by A. J. Brooks. Carroll's colleague Frederick York Powell marked the auction with a poem that begins:

> Poor playthings of the man that's gone,
> Surely we would not have them thrown,
> Like wreckage on a barren strand,
> The prey of every greedy hand.

In June 1898, items from the Brooks auction reappeared for sale in a catalog of secondhand books at B.H. Blackwell in Oxford, as well as in a catalog of The Art and Antiques Agency in Oxford and in two other 1898 sales.

It is reasonable to declare that the season for collecting Lewis Carroll began at that first major 1898 auction by Brooks. Items from it were bought, sold, reauctioned, and dispersed worldwide – many of them resurfacing in the collections described in this volume. Some items by the world-famous author were collected and hidden away in private collections. One such item, for example, was the now-famous suppressed "The Wasp in a Wig" episode from *Through the Looking-Glass* that was known to exist but was long thought lost and probably destroyed. It did not appear by name in the 1898 auction, but it suddenly appeared at a Sotheby's Parke-Bernet London auction in 1974, identified as being purchased at the Brooks auction in 1898. It became known later that the "gentleman" who consigned the edited galley proofs had inherited them from a member of his family. Clearly, it was "collected."

One might think the purchaser was among the very first Carroll collectors, yet there were many already in 1898. Indeed, the Schaefer Collection described in this book was begun in 1892 in the United States.

It, like many, began as an *Alice* collection. *Alice* collections and Carroll collections are not always the same thing, especially when it comes to items other than books. A collection of book editions of the *Alice*s published in Carroll's lifetime is one kind of Alice collection, but a collection of figurines, including Christmas ornaments, modeled on characters in the *Alice* books is something else…a Carroll collection or an *Alice* collection? Add in figures from the Disney *Alices*, and what kind of collection is it? Plus, the earliest collections surely were relatively small and mostly consisted of Carroll's works published in his lifetime – not at all like today's large collections with thousands of items.

Alice at age eight, photographed by Carroll

Collectors rely on checklists and bibliographies. Carroll's nephew Stuart Dodgson Collingwood's 1898 biography, *The Life and Letters of Lewis Carroll (Rev. C. L. Dodgson)*, contained the first published bibliography of the works of Lewis Carroll, marking it as the first checklist of Carroll items for future collectors to work from. The bibliography contained only publications, but the lavishly illustrated text made wide reference to photographs, manuscripts, letters, and association items.

In 1924, a second bibliography – the mark of active interest in collecting Carroll – was compiled by Sidney Herbert Williams and published as *A Bibliography of the Writings of Lewis Carroll*. Next, in 1931, Falconer Madan expanded Williams's reference work into *A Handbook of the Literature of the Works of the Rev. C. L. Dodgson (Lewis Carroll)*. It was updated in 1962 by Roger Lancelyn Green and in 1979 by Denis Crutch.

♥
Alice Liddell Hargreaves in 1932, at age eighty
♥

By the 1960s and 1970s, the afterlife of Carroll and his works far exceeded his initial output. Starting when the copyright expired on *Alice's Adventures in Wonderland* in 1907, the number of new editions with different formats and often new illustrations by various hands changed the world of Carroll collecting. Films emerged. Translations grew geometrically. Association items of all shapes and kinds were marketed. In 2024, a vastly updated *Charles Lutwidge Dodgson (Lewis Carroll): A Bibliography of Works Published in His Lifetime* was compiled by Charlie Lovett for the Lewis Carroll Society of North America (LCSNA) as a definitive reference for Carroll publications during Carroll's lifetime.

For the book world of the *Alices*, extending far beyond Carroll's lifetime and extending far beyond publications in Great Britain and America, Jon Lindseth launched a global initiative that resulted in 2023 in the massive two-volume edition *Alice in a World of Wonderlands: The English Language Editions of the Four Alice Books*. This is a somewhat companion volume to an earlier Lindseth project on translations of the *Alice*s completed by many hands, also published in two large volumes: *Alice in a World of Wonderlands: The Translations of Lewis Carroll's Masterpiece* (2015).

For the non-book world of Carroll collecting, the Internet has become the go-to source for items, led by eBay and Etsy and Joel Birenbaum's Alice in Wonderland Collectors Network. The LCSNA's semiannual *Knight Letter* publication and online blog have proven equally valuable sources of timely information and historic records.

Alice Was a Curious Child

Who was the first great Carroll collection and collector? A convincing case can be made for it being the real Alice herself. At her request, Carroll wrote and gave Alice Liddell the manuscript book of *Alice's Adventures Under Ground,* which she held in her collection until, as Mrs. Reginald Hargreaves, she chose to sell it in 1928 to help pay estate taxes when her husband died. Carroll, of course, also gave her a first edition of *Alice's Adventures in Wonderland*, and in 1869 a copy of the first German translation of *Wonderland*, bound in green Morocco leather, and the first French translation, bound in red Morocco leather, and copies of his other books. But beyond the items Carroll gave her and the letters he wrote to her, she both actively collected Carroll items and memorabilia and preserved them as a collection – which, as reported by her biographer, Anne Clark, in *The Real Alice,* she kept locked in her private study.

Beyond possessing cherished first editions of "almost everything" Carroll had written and many mementos, after Carroll's death Alice "demonstrated her continued interest in her adventures by collecting new editions as they appeared. She loved fine illustrations, though she never saw any she liked so well as those of Tenniel," according to Clarke. "But the new additions to her collection that she prized most were the foreign editions, translations into more languages than she could ever have imagined on that golden afternoon when the story was first told."

The sale of the *Under Ground* manuscript at Sotheby's on June 11, 1928, included other Carroll items, but not the whole collection. When Alice passed away in 1934, her remaining Carroll collection of books, items, and memorabilia was inherited by her son, Caryl Hargreaves. It was not until his passing in 1955 that the collection was further dispersed through donations and sales. Hargreaves donated letters from Carroll to Alice to the British Museum (now in the museum's British Library), and many of the Carroll items owned by Alice were spread worldwide, sold and resold, and are represented today in major institutional and private collections, including many in this volume.

But like the gift that keeps giving, Sotheby's held an auction it called Lewis Carroll's Alice: The Photographs,

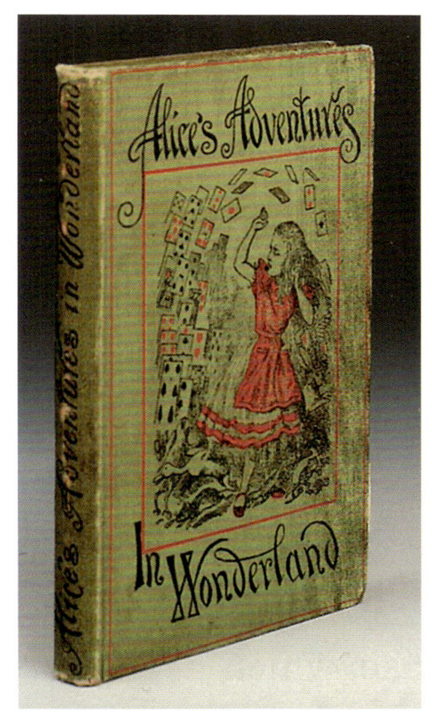

Alice's copy of the 1896 46th thousand Macmillan "People's Edition" of *Alice's Adventures in Wonderland*, signed by Alice P. Hargreaves

Alice's copy of the 1898 48th thousand Macmillan "People's Edition" of *Through the Looking-Glass*

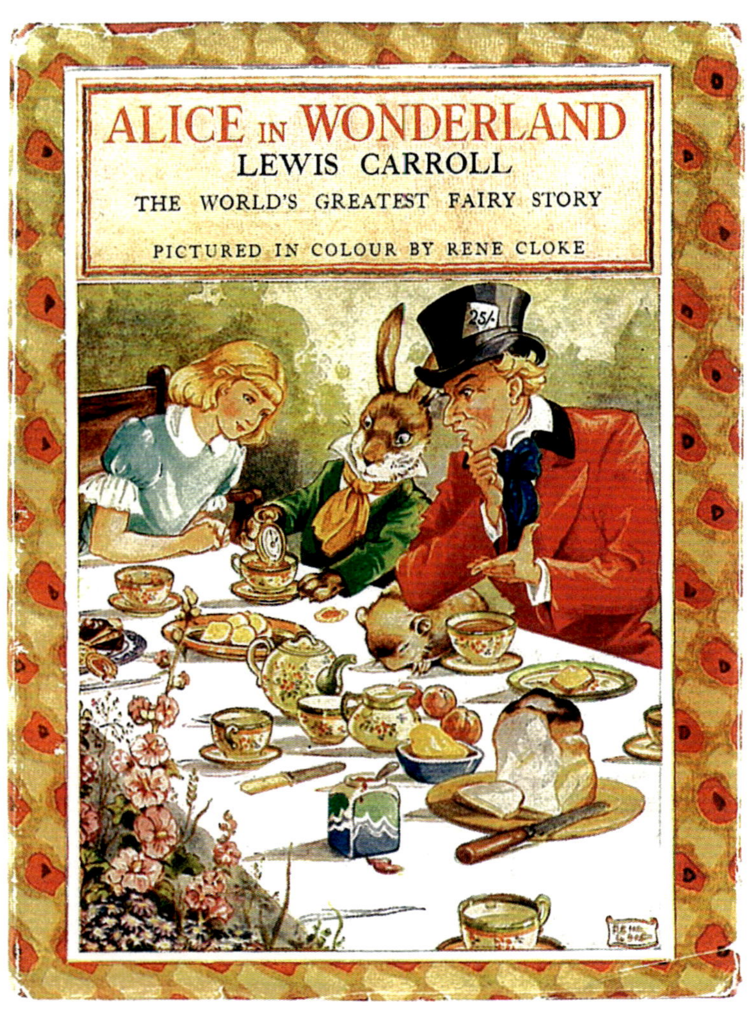

Books, Papers and Personal Effects of Alice Liddell and Her Family, on June 6, 2001. It seems Caryl Hargreaves and other members of Alice's family had stored archival material at Christ Church, Oxford, and Caryl's daughter decided to finally sell it off. The extensive offerings included Alice's photograph scrapbook, which included forty-eight images by Carroll, letters to and from Carroll, and the white vellum copy of the facsimile edition of *Alice's Adventures Under Ground* that Carroll gave her, inscribed, "to Her whose namesake on one happy summer day inspired this story." The sale contained the two George IV mahogany bookcases that housed Alice's collection. Almost all the editions and translations of the *Alice* books she collected were signed. Even a few parodies and pastiches made it into her holdings.

The many items reaffirmed Alice's lifelong interest and pride in things Carrollian. One book, presented in 1889 to her son Alan (who died in 1915), is inscribed: "Alan… from his mother, 'Alice in Wonderland.'" As noted, Alice was especially fond of translations of the *Alice* books. The Sotheby 2001 auction contained thirty-four translations of *Alice* and two of *Looking-Glass* in a total of seventeen languages. Twenty-seven of the translations were signed by Alice. Among them was Alice's copy of Vladimir Nabokov's 1923 translation of *Alice* into Russian – a collector's prize indeed. But another lot demonstrates the breadth and passion of Alice, the first major Lewis Carroll collector: eighty-seven mostly illustrated editions of the

Alice books collected by Alice and her son Caryl Hargreaves.

The person who can be regarded as the first major collector and leader of the parade of the great Carroll collectors of the 20th century was the American Harcourt Amory (1845–1915), whose collection now resides in the Houghton Library at Harvard University. Another American, Morris L. Parrish (1865–1944), also amassed major holdings of Carroll books and materials, including some of Carroll's photograph albums. Today they are housed amid his collection of Victorian novelists at Princeton University.

Illustrated editions in the Alice Liddell Hargreaves Collection

Other great collectors include Eldridge Johnson (whose collection is included among other Carroll collections in the New York Public Library Berg Collection [Johnson purchased the original manuscript of *Under Ground* when Alice Hargreaves sold it in 1928]); A.S.W. Rosenbach (a book dealer whose collection resides at The Rosenbach in Philadelphia); Arthur Houghton (his collection now resides at the Morgan Library in New York); Warren Weaver (his comprehensive collection, which includes extensive photograph albums and translations, is housed at the Harry Ransom Humanities Research Center at the University of Texas at Austin); and Alfred Berol (housed at New York University). Add to those the Carroll collection at the Lilly Library at Indiana University.

Of special note is that all these libraries mentioned in the prior two paragraphs are in the United States and have a copy of the *Alice* edition of all *Alice* editions – the withdrawn 1865 *Alice's Adventures in Wonderland*,

♥

Illustrated editions in the Alice Liddell Hargreaves Collection

♥

of which only six copies remain in private hands. Also of special note is the story of the manuscript of *Under Ground* – from Carroll's gift to Alice Liddell, to her sale of it at public auction in 1928 to cover the estate taxes after her husband's death, to its purchase by the American book dealer Rosenbach, who sold it to the collector Johnson. Upon Johnson's death in 1946, it was put up for auction again and purchased by a group of wealthy American benefactors (some of whom are named above), who arranged for its dramatic return in 1948 to the British people (it is currently housed in the British Library) "as an expression of thanks to a noble people who held Hitler at bay for a long period single-handed."

Relevant to public collections in this book on private collections is that some collectors gain added pleasure and perhaps justification in creating holdings that support scholarship, science, and art. That is certainly true of the Wakeling Collection and the Lovett Collection described in this book, both of which, beyond Carroll items, contain extensive research materials on Victorian people and culture relevant to the study of Carroll and his world. It is also true of the Cassady Collection, which was donated to the University of Southern California in 2000 and is used for the annual Wonderland awards for collegiate scholarship and creative works inspired by the collection and the works of Lewis Carroll.

Over the years, major collectors have not only aspired to have their collections remain intact, but have sought university homes so their holdings could be visited by serious students and enthusiasts. That is what happened to the outstanding Carroll collection amassed in the last half of the 20th century by Joseph Brabant, a Canadian. In 1997, the Brabant Collection was donated to the University of Toronto and is now housed in the Thomas Fisher Rare Book Library at the university.

Toward a Taxonomy of Collections and an Appreciation of Collecting

How does one explain what a Carroll collection is and what categories of items are collected? Most Carroll collections through the years have been built upon texts, whether restricted to just the *Alice* books or more comprehensively to all of Carroll's publications and manuscripts. It is safe to say that Carroll collectors have a love for books. But in this increasingly digitized and merchandized world, today's collections include a lot more than books. Some specialized collections, in fact, can have but a few books.

It should be noted generally about collecting that it requires money – a little discretionary money, or a lot. And while collections of rare items chosen wisely can be good investments, no one gets rich quickly collecting

Lewis Carroll. Solid collections with rare items can appreciate over time, but "making money" was not a motivator for the collectors in this volume. (The drivers of value in a collection generally are rarity, provenance, and condition.) Nor was the drive for status or prestige a motivator, in the way it can be reflected in collections of, say, watches or automobiles or 19th-century French paintings or yachts. Certainly, the collectors in this volume are proud of their collections and people are impressed with their holdings…often awed. But first editions of *Sylvie and Bruno* and *Sylvie and Bruno Concluded* just don't impress the way collections of diamond jewelry do.

Strictly speaking, analysis means taking the whole and breaking it into parts. So how does one analyze a Carroll collection? For the sake of simplicity, and to broadly describe the nature of current Carroll collections, we can break it into four buckets or tiers. Half the tiers track to Carroll's lifetime and the other half, obviously, thereafter. So that is a dividing line for items in a Carroll collection. Back to value and rarity, there are plenty of reprints of Macmillan editions of the *Alice* books from Carroll's lifetime. As with Dickens's most popular novels, there were so many initial copies printed and then reprinted that they are not particularly rare or unaffordably expensive for most people. But rarities such as the first impression, first printing of Carroll's works in his lifetime, signed dedication copies, or copies owned by his close friends, are increasingly hard to find and valuable, as are his autographed letters and other edited manuscripts, corrected proofs of his books, and his photographs. One of the key reasons they are increasingly rare for a collector is that many have passed into permanent collections in institutions and are thus off the market.

These rare primary Carroll items from his lifetime would populate that first tier. So too would all the non-first printings of his books with very minor text changes be part of this primary category, as they have been throughout the history of Lewis Carroll collections. And they are a core component of traditional collections. All the major collections profiled in this volume contain a traditional core component. Carroll helped his future collectors by being a dedicated inscriber, known for penning his name or a "from the author" dedication on close to two thousand books and photographs.

Tier two is also restricted to objects from Carroll's lifetime, including a range of association items, from books Carroll owned or those owned by someone connected to him; some furniture and objects he possessed; items published about Carroll, including reviews and even his obituaries; and materials related to his photography or theatrical productions of *Alice* and related theater interests. Correspondence mentioning him would also fall into this category. Again, the associative nature of all of these – even when not connected directly to his literary or artistic works – opens a world of connections, lives, and stories.

Tiers three and four are where the evolution of Carroll collecting in the 20th and 21st centuries is demonstrated in all its permutations and could debatably and perhaps absurdly be expanded to many tiers. Again, for simplicity's sake, let's define tier three as containing text objects; as such, it includes many English-language editions of Carroll's works, as well as translations published around the world, including the waves of post-Tenniel editions illustrated by other artists (as long as they include the text of Carroll's work). It also includes the increasingly large area of scholarship written on Carroll's life and works.

That would leave the vast category of objects inspired by Carroll's works, such as films and other works of visual art and music, as well as associated pins and teapots, ephemera, and other such "collectibles," as tier four (admittedly, at times a strange wonderland of remotely connected items, but all true Carrolliana).

Another way of looking at what people are collecting, beyond the traditional items from Carroll's lifetime, is by example: parodies, spin-offs, imitations, plays, ballets, radio and spoken recordings, films and television, excerpts published separately or in anthologies, biographies and criticism, posters, advertisements, translations, illustrated editions, postcards, stamps, pottery, dolls, and more. See the Tannenbaum Collection for a sense of what a contemporary "completist and peripheralist" collection contains, including Alice pinball machines.

Carroll's Cheshire Cat famously said, "We're all mad here." And while building significant Carroll collections may seem odd to some, is it any madder than collecting, say, vinyl record albums, thimbles, baseball cards, comic books, dolls, old soda bottles and cans, or fifty of the familiar things that seemingly "normal" people collect? There is always more that can be said about a human behavior as complex as collecting. "The attempt to understand collecting not only adds to our knowledge of human nature but also enhances the experience of collecting itself," asserts G. Thomas Tanselle, who adds, "One's sense of self-awareness is increased by being able to place one's own endeavors in a framework that comprehends the full panoply of related pursuits." Hardly mad behavior.

Overall, collecting items relating to the life and work of Lewis Carroll isn't particularly odd. The human drive for order and the thrill of chance are part of the collecting gene, as is a curiosity about things, especially from the past – and not only curiosity but a desire to understand them and their place in the continuum. Probably this is all evident in another common feeling expressed by many of the collectors interviewed for this book: the thrill and connection of being in the moment with Lewis Carroll; the emotional connection, when holding one of the books he owned, or a letter he penned. It's one form of a collector's high.

Things and objects one loved as a child won't make you young again, but nostalgia is a common experience and often triggers feelings of personal happiness and comfort. Many of the collectors in this volume expressed what can be called nostalgic feelings about Alice in their childhoods that carry through to their collecting experiences and their collection.

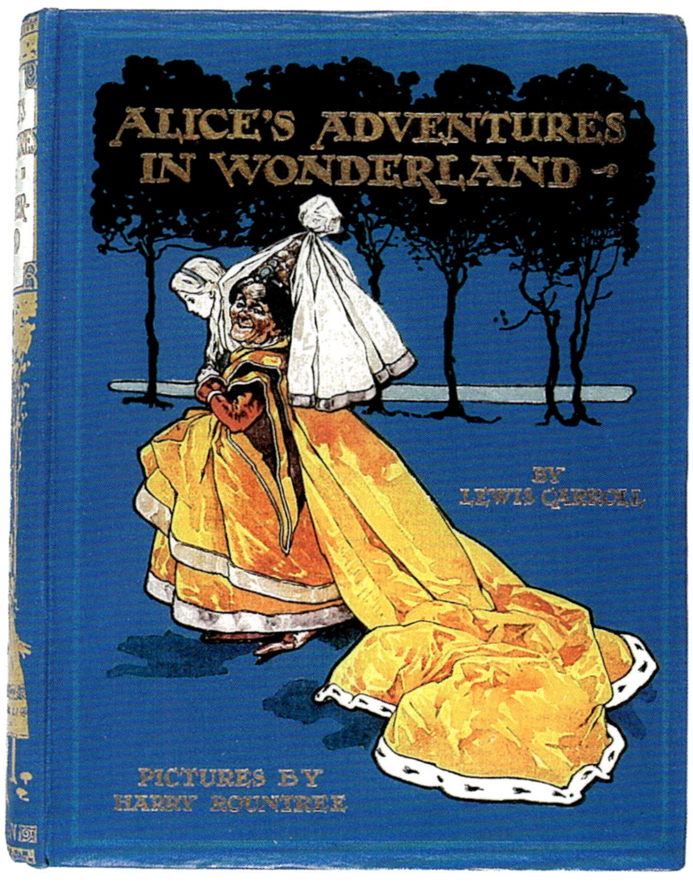

A Collection's Fate

The fun of the hunt, the discoveries, the cataloging, the filling in of gaps, the holding and reviewing the items in a collection, the camaraderie of like-minded collectors, the collaboration… this is but a partial list of the pleasures of collecting. But collections lead to the inevitable question of what happens to the collection when a collector either no longer wants it or has passed away.

There are several paths most collectors take. One is passing the collection to a relative who is interested in continuing the collection or some part of it. Such is the case with family collections such as the Burstein Collection (father to son) and the Schaefer Collection (grandmother to son to granddaughter). That is not an option for many collectors. And it is not a likely option in perpetuity.

It isn't all that surprising that some simply ignore any thoughts of or plans for disposition. "I don't want to think about it," is perhaps understandable, and pushing away a decision is human. The collection is part of their life; they live with it and don't want to imagine living without it. Presumably, they figure their estate will do something with it and they don't care what, or don't care to know what. The executors of some estates are banks and lawyers who,

ALICE'S ADVENTURES
IN WONDERLAND

Book from the Alice Liddell Hargreaves collection auctioned in 2001

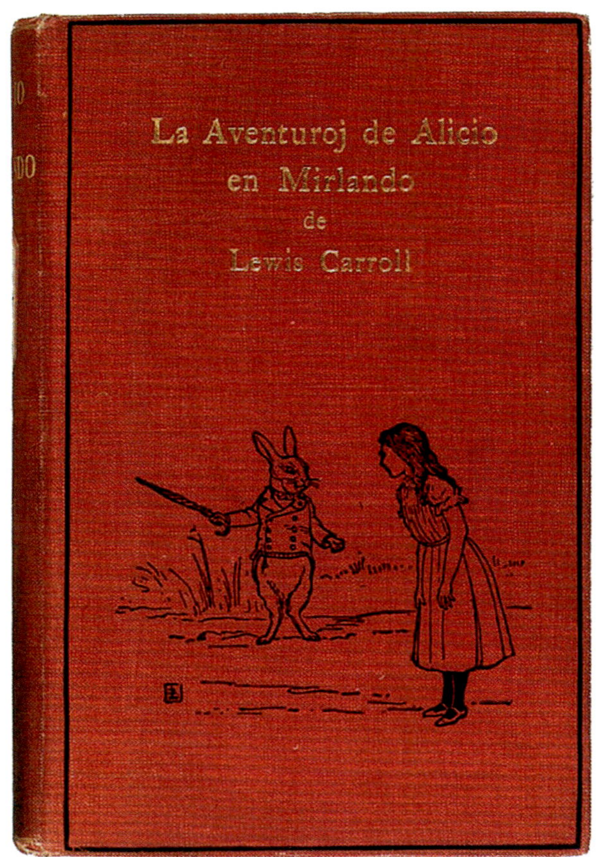

♥

Books from the Alice Liddell Hargreaves collection auctioned in 2001

♥

absent any written instruction, just liquidate the collection. Thus, an "estate sale." Similarly, when a collection is no longer being maintained, including inherited collections, it may still be passed to a family member for disposition, often for the shared benefit of the family or heirs. After nearly two-thirds of a century, that's what happened to the real Alice's collection. So either money is generated at some point and spread to the inheritors, or items in the collection are spread around, or both.

The sincerest wish of many collectors is to keep their collection intact, as they had built it. The idea of a tangible testimonial to their life and efforts is appealing. The two possible destinations are another private collection or an institutional collection. Keeping a collection together and having it bear one's name can be a motivation to collect. However, today many major book and author collections are not accepted by nonprofit institutions unless they come with an endowment, or at least a contribution for cataloging and organizing the donated holdings. The large Wakeling Collection was donated to the Surrey History Centre. As noted earlier, the Cassady Collection was donated to the Libraries of the University of Southern California. The Lindseth Collection is destined for several locations – to Oxford University to fill a conspicuous gap in its holdings, but elsewhere as well; for example, more than seven hundred and fifty of the collection's illustrated editions are already at the rare book library at Case Western Reserve University.

♥

Rare 1893 *Through the Looking-Glass* biscuit tin used by Alice and her family

♥

A further disposition path is arguably a noble one. A collector may want to move on to building another collection, or simply auction off or otherwise sell their holdings and perhaps even admire the items' new homes. A key motivation then is to return the items to the market so others can seek and enjoy them. This is what happened late in 2023, for example, to the fine Lewis Carroll and Alice Collection of Stephen and Nancy Farber. It was auctioned off in Chicago, with Stephen remarking in the catalog that after forty-five years, "It seems appropriate to return these items to Alice enthusiasts."

The collections described in the pages that follow are outstanding achievements worthy of much admiration and appreciation. They reflect the art of collecting, boundless curiosity, self-expression, and specific knowledge that signifies humanity. Their stories merit telling and memorializing in a frozen moment in time: 2024.

THE Birenbaum COLLECTION

It could be said it began – as it did for many Lewis Carroll aficionados of the late 20th and early 21st centuries – with a copy of *The Annotated Alice*. In Joel Birenbaum's case, the book was recommended to this future engineer in his junior year of high school by an English teacher at the famed Brooklyn Tech High School. "It was a magical experience for me; finally a book I could identify with," recalls Joel. "After all, Carroll was a mathematician and a logician who was adept in his art of wordplay. I love a good puzzle."

It might also be said it began with the Salvador Dali-illustrated edition of *Alice's Adventures in Wonderland*, a nearly obligatory and expensive volume in all major collections – but surely before and after Joel Birenbaum, never the first book in a Carroll collection. Chance or fate reigned when Joel was twenty-six years old and working for Western Electric. "I went to talk to a colleague about a project. He was on the phone, so I sat down and picked up his *Chicago Sun Times* (a newspaper I never read) and looked through the classified ads and found someone offering a limited-edition *Alice* illustrated by Salvador Dali and signed by him on the frontispiece. It was way more than I would spend for a book, but I did some research and found that the price was more than reasonable, so I held my breath and purchased it. I was not yet a collector."

BEGUN
1978

SIZE
7,709 items
(plus "googobs of stuff")

SCOPE
Comprehensive

HIGHLIGHTS
First and rare editions, illustrated *Alices*, three-dimensional items, original artwork, translations

The Carroll collector switch in his head clicked on when his sister-in-law, a collector and library science professor, learned about Joel's Dali purchase and his affinity for *Alice*. She suggested he collect illustrated *Alices*. "I had no clue what she was talking about," Joel admits. "She then informed me of a book titled *The Illustrators of Alice* by Graham Ovenden and John Davis that had a list of 156 illustrated *Alices*. An engineer with a list is a force of nature. From that moment on I was a man on a mission."

But he was an inexperienced book collector finding his way and passion, and the growth of his collection was woefully slow. He frequented local used bookstores and

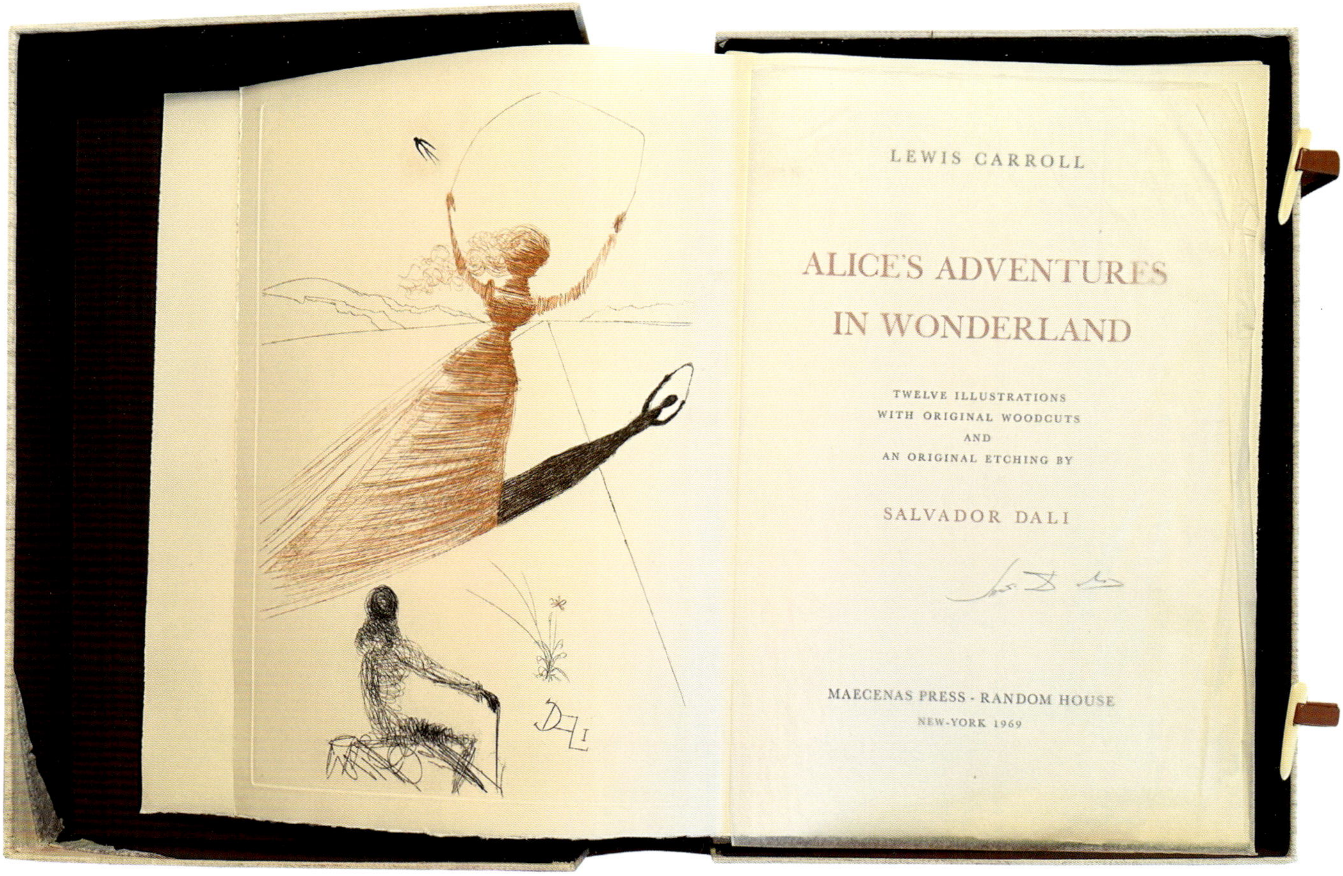

LEWIS CARROLL

ALICE'S ADVENTURES IN WONDERLAND

TWELVE ILLUSTRATIONS
WITH ORIGINAL WOODCUTS
AND
AN ORIGINAL ETCHING BY

SALVADOR DALI

MAECENAS PRESS - RANDOM HOUSE
NEW-YORK 1969

The Dali *Alice* (frontispiece, top, and down the rabbit hole, bottom). It was released in 1969 and contained 12 illustrations by Dali—one for each chapter, plus a cover. It quickly sold out.

Alice
au pays des merveilles
Illustrations
d'Adrienne Ségur
flammarion

flea markets, which grew his holdings to twenty-five books. One of his earliest finds was a prepublication unbound copy of *Alice*, illustrated by Ralph Steadman (perhaps best known for his collaborations with Hunter S. Thompson).

Joel's journey from a collector of illustrated *Alices* to a collector of all things Carrollian took off when he joined the Lewis Carroll Society of North America (LCSNA). In 1980, Joel relates, "I attended a local book auction and purchased a copy of *The Wasp in a Wig*, published by the Lewis Carroll Society of North America and edited by Edward Guiliano, which contained the contact information for the society's secretary, Maxine Schaefer." So he joined, and with Schaefer's help was quickly welcomed by a network of collectors, starting with Byron Sewell and Alice Berkey. A previously planned trip to Britain led to meetings with Edward Wakeling, Selwyn Goodacre, and Catherine and Mark Richards, as well as considerable additions of items and ideas for his collection. "Book collecting is not a competition," Joel understood.

More than forty years later, the Birenbaum Collection contains nearly all of the 156 illustrated editions on his initial checklist. Deciding on what would come next, Joel listened to the counsel of collector August Imholtz. August asked him why he didn't collect translations of *Alice*. Joel replied that it didn't make sense to collect books he couldn't read. August asked him if he had read all the *Alice* books that were on his shelves. "My collection was focused on different illustrators; therefore, it made perfect sense to collect foreign editions illustrated by illustrators from that country, and a new horizon opened to my search," Joel says. "It helped that I was on a work project that provided the opportunity for international travel. My initial translation collection was strong in Dutch, Korean, Arabic, Hebrew, and Chinese, for that reason. With the aid of illustrator Maxim Mitrofanov, who I met via the Alice in Wonderland Collectors Network, I have greatly expanded

♥

Adrienne Ségur's illustrated French edition of *Alice's Adventures in Wonderland* (1949)

♥

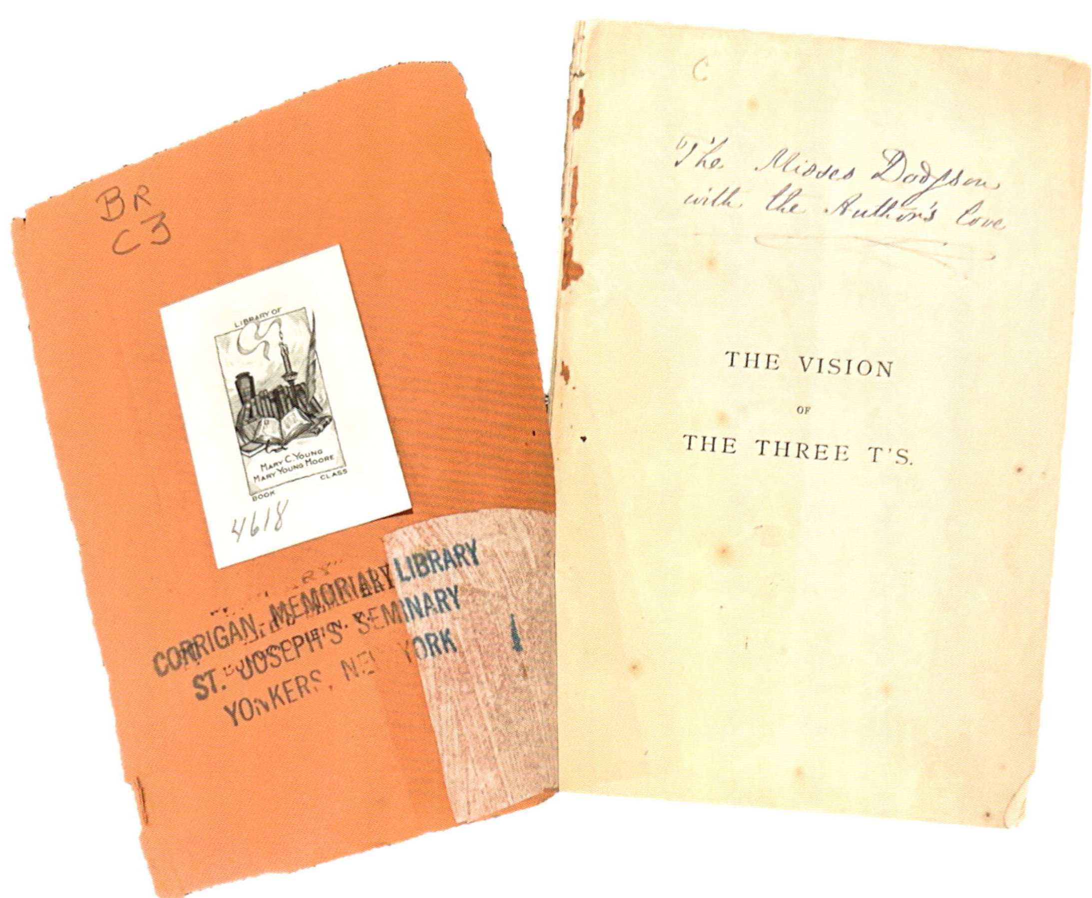

♥

Presentation copy of *The Vision of the Three T's* (1873), inscribed by the author to "The Misses Dodgson," his sisters

♥

my holdings of Russian editions. Also, new French, German, and Japanese books were readily available in the United States." The Birenbaum Collection currently contains copies of 492 translations "and more coming."

Joel continued to add to his database of illustrated and non-illustrated editions, so that today the Birenbaum Collection contains 2,239 books, including *Alices* (818 copies), parodies, biographies, literary criticisms, other reference books, and other books written by Carroll. However, it is the 5,470 other items in his collection that truly distinguishes it. Still, the books – and not just the translations and illustrated editions – are impressive.

"Every so often, the universe smiles on a determined collector," says Joel. He placed a free ad in a weekly antiques publication, looking for an 1866 *Alice* and other older editions, and "out of the blue" he was offered a first edition of *Alice's Adventures Under Ground*, from a convent. At one point, he was contacted by a library to see if he was interested in a collection of Alice memorabilia.

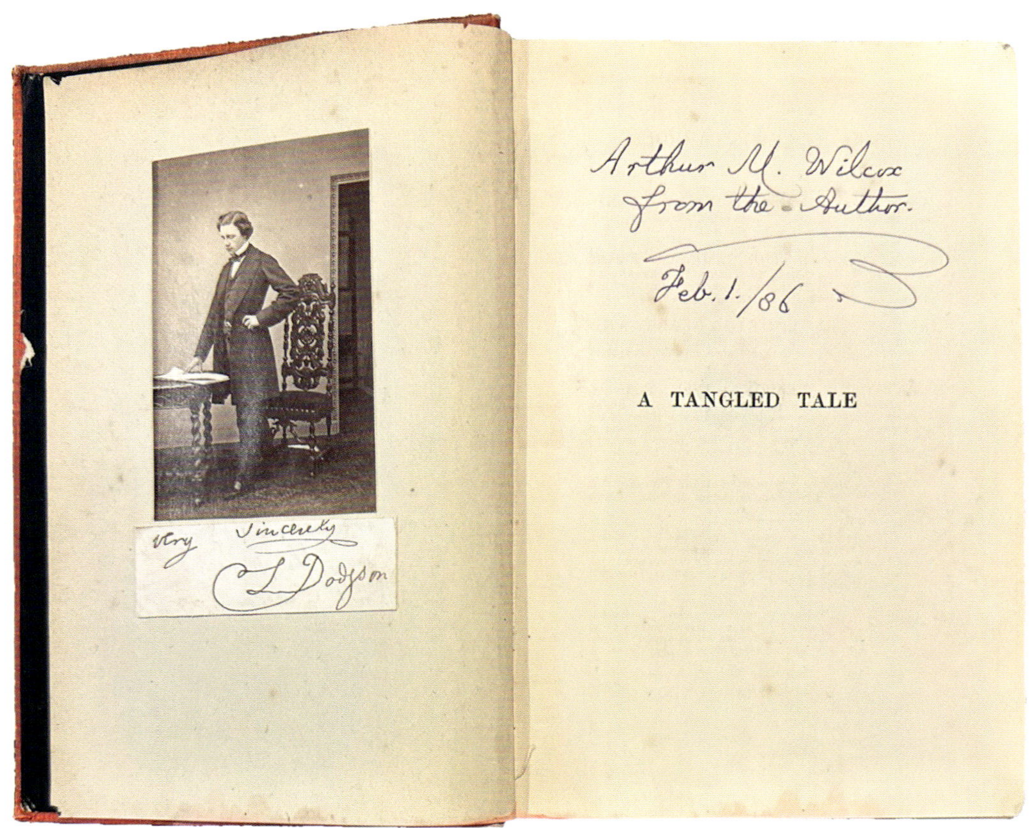

A Tangled Tale, inscribed by the author in 1886

They sent photos, "we came to an agreement, and I bought it." Still later, he was offered an Appleton *Alice*; it was not in great condition, "but it was good enough for me, since I never thought I would own one."

Once through a friend he found out a local Chicago book dealer, James Borg, was putting his stock up for auction. Joel attended that weekend sale and came home with copies of *The Vision of the Three T's* (ex libris) inscribed by Carroll to his sisters, *Syzygies and Lanrick* (ex libris) with author's corrections, and *The Game of Logic*. "I couldn't believe my overall luck." Amusingly, the presentation copy of *The Vision of the Three T's* had spent time in the library of a seminary in New York.

On another occasion, he found a first edition of *A Tangled Tale,* inscribed to "Arthur M. Wilcox from the Author," in the Marshall Fields rare book room. "It was priced way more than I wanted to pay, as it had a water stain on the front cover, but to its credit, it also had an original photo tipped in, and another tipped-in piece underneath signed 'Sincerely C.L. Dodgson.' I visited this book three times over a six-month period before I broke down and purchased it." Another special book prized by Joel is an 1891 copy of *The Hunting of the Snark,* which is an association copy that belonged to W.W. Denslow, who illustrated *The Wonderful Wizard of Oz.* "It is something that impresses those who are collectors of both Oz and Wonderland."

Another book that holds a special place in his heart is the pop-up *Alice* book illustrated by Vojtech Kubasta, "which my son, Josh, bought for me at a flea market while searching for Star Wars collectibles. We would often attend flea markets together, and it was a great pleasure to watch him bargain with sellers while exhibiting the same mannerisms and tactics that I did. I asked him what he paid for it, and he told me five dollars. At the time it was listed for one hundred fifty dollars, but he didn't know that."

Beyond Books

When Joel started collecting memorabilia, he simply considered what he calls his Alice "stuff" as accent pieces to be displayed with his book collection. Over time he realized he was collecting Alice items that were all representative of her presence in the popular culture. He believes this is important because it is testament to the impact of the original books. *Alice* is still relevant in the everyday life of the general public so many years after its publication – something Joel calls "a rare feat" and deserving of a place in his collection. These memorabilia and ephemera now number more than 5,000 pieces in the Birenbaum Collection. They include figurines, teapots and tea sets, toys, games, paintings, sculptures, Christmas ornaments, dolls, action figures, nutcrackers, tins, postcards, greeting cards, music boxes, games, fabrics, newspaper articles, magazines, watches, tchotchkes, and

Graham Piggott's *Cheshire Cat*, with the features of Joel Birenbaum, ca. 1999

Joel with a few shelves of frowning and grinning characters he has collected

more miscellaneous "stuff." His three-dimensional items are a highlight of the collection.

A signature item is a Graham Piggott sculpture he commissioned of the Cheshire Cat with the features of Joel's face. "I was in his studio in Bladen purchasing another one of his Alice sculptures [there are six in the Birenbaum Collection], when he asked me to sit down so he could make a model of my face in clay. While he was working on that, we chatted most engagingly about our connections with Alice. My enduring friendship with the talented sculptor Graham and his wife, Corri, continues to this day."

Another work of art with pride of place in the Birenbaum Collection is a set of twenty-seven watercolor paintings he acquired between 2009 and 2015 of characters from the *Alice* books by Dominic Murphy. Joel first discovered Murphy on eBay. "I am so enamored with his style that I have fifteen of his paintings hanging on the wall going up the staircase to my Carroll library, and I refer to it as my family portrait wall." That staircase is in Joel's current home in New Bern, North Carolina, where he is retired. When he lived in suburban Chicago, the collection room was a spare bedroom. Its current dedicated space is three times the size of that bedroom, and some items find their way up the stairs and on walls elsewhere in the house, as well.

Associated with the collection are still more "googobs of stuff" from a prodigious Carroll life of connections. Joel served as president of the LCSNA for four years in the 1980s. In the late 1980s, he formed the Alice in Wonderland Collectors Network, with which he is still well connected. There were originally twenty members of this group, and at first Joel collected lists of Alice items for sale, compiled information on new items that became commercially available, and distributed the finished product via U.S. mail. It has evolved into a Facebook group with more than 13,000 members.

Dominic Murphy's
Cheshire Cat, ca. 2012

Joel has organized many exhibits and programs over the years, including the Alice 150 ten-day extravaganza in New York City in 2015. In 1990, he "encouraged" a large exhibition at the Newberry Library in Chicago – 125 Years of Alice's Adventures in Wonderland: A Collector's Perspective. The Newberry provided two display cases showing some highlights of their collection, including a prized 1865 first edition of *Alice*, first editions of *Through the Looking-Glass* and *Alice's Adventures Under Ground*, five Dalziel Brothers engravings, and one original John Tenniel drawing. Joel curated thirteen cases of items from his personal collection, including many items reflecting Carroll in the popular culture. The exhibition was a great success, visited by classes of schoolchildren and the general public. Two moments he saw during the exhibition touched him deeply. "I saw an octogenarian woman viewing a case that brought tears to her eyes because of memories she was reliving. The second was witnessing a young child, standing on tiptoes on a two-step stair, smiling joyfully while looking at a case of pop-up books. This is why I collect *Alice*. It verifies my belief that *Alice* remains relevant over 150 years after its publication."

At age seventy-seven, Joel is still actively collecting, mostly online. The thrill of the hunt before the Internet has been replaced by the joy of acquiring things that would be impossible to find without it. "I am always surprised to learn about items for sale or simply in existence that I've never heard about; there's still so much in all sorts of Alice categories."

His current thinking is that the Birenbaum Collection will eventually be donated to an institution "that really wants it." But, he adds, "I have often said that my collection of fellow Alice collectors is my most valuable one." He attributes his success in collecting to the experience gained while viewing the private and personal collections of serious collectors. "Sharing my knowledge and exhibiting Alice stuff are continuing sources of joy."

THE

Burstein

COLLECTION

It is not unreasonable to assert that the extensive, multigenerational Burstein Collection began in Sandor Burstein's nursery back in 1928 – though the conscious collection start date is 1976. Back in the day, Sandor's mother, Lottie, covered the walls of her children's bedroom with *Alice in Wonderland* wallpaper. Sandor was four years old. Today, that very wallpaper and matched curtains hold pride of place as the items with the most sentimental value among the more than six thousand objects lovingly amassed in the Burstein Collection: rare and popular editions of Lewis Carroll's works, translations, biographies, bibliographies, collections of letters, abridgements, diaries, parodies, comics, pastiches, marginalia, fiction, catalogs, anthologies, academia, hermeneutica, dramas, annotations, interpretations, books about Carroll's photography and mathematics, Carroll illustrators, original art, and a few thousand tchotchkes, toys, dolls, and other non-book items.

Another item of great personal significance and sentimental value is the book that started it all: an edition of *Alice's Adventures in Wonderland* in Portuguese. Not only is it the first Carroll book officially "collected" by Sandor, but it is also the first translation in the collection, which son Mark Burstein has grown to 153 languages – a distinguishing characteristic in a collection with several extraordinary characteristics.

Sandor, a distinguished physician in San Francisco, had a lifelong affinity for Carroll and his *Alice,* which included falling in love with his schoolteacher, Miss Kathleen Sherman, who played Alice (and the White Rabbit) in a local production. Sandor was enchanted, and often professed that his love for all things Alice traced back to that golden afternoon of theater in 1934. Later, he wrote several papers on Carroll in college, but Alice remained in the background for much of his life, until he began to pursue her on his world travels.

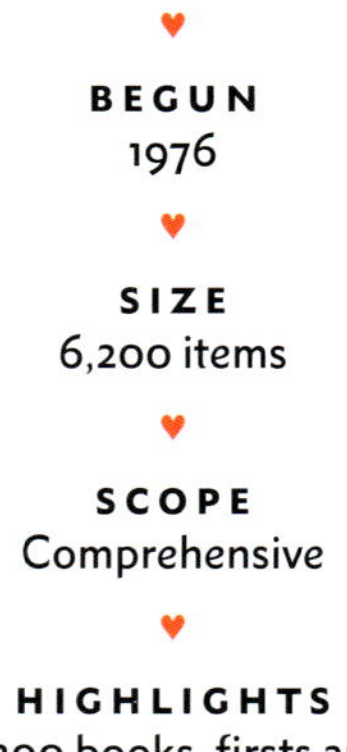

♥

BEGUN
1976

♥

SIZE
6,200 items

♥

SCOPE
Comprehensive

♥

HIGHLIGHTS
4,200 books, firsts and association copies, translations in 153 languages, comics, original art, illustrated editions

♥

Wallpaper and textile

The Burstein collection

On one of his frequent trips abroad, he thought to himself, "It would be fun to collect one edition of the same book from every country I travel to, and *Alice* is one I always recognize." So, when he was in Portugal in 1976, he made the fateful purchase of a Portuguese edition of *Alice*. That purchase amuses Mark today, because he discovered that this "seed" book had been published in Brazil, not Portugal.

Once Sandor's patients and friends noticed his assortment of *Alice* materials, they started giving him *Alice* books, and one day he realized he was collecting. He started going to bookstores, antiquarian book fairs, and other sources for Carroll items. It did not take long for Mark, in his twenties, to start tagging along to join the hunt. Theirs was a mutual collection, with each Burstein contributing to it.

Sandor had given Mark a copy of *The Annotated Alice* when he was ten, and Mark was and continues to be fascinated by everything in and about it (in fact, he expanded and updated the 150th Anniversary Deluxe Edition in 2015). Like father, like son, Mark went on to write papers on Carroll and his works in college. For him, it was at the University of California at Santa Cruz. And, like his father, he went on to become a president of the Lewis Carroll Society of North America (LCSNA).

Miss Kathleen Sherman

Portuguese edition of *Alice* published by Edições Melhoramentos

Mark is also a prolific author and editor of all things Carrollian. From the collection's earliest days, he was all in. Their "mutual collection" changed homes in 1999 when Sandor moved to a smaller home and his Alice room was already looking a bit like John Tenniel's version of Alice in W. RABBIT'S HOUSE (Chapter IV) and echoing a certain chorus of "No room! No room!" That's when Sandor gave possession of the Burstein Collection to Mark.

Association Items

As is true for all the major collections in this book, the collector always wants to and succeeds in owning items that the author, Charles Lutwidge Dodgson, held in his hands. In addition to letters, inscribed books, a Carroll photograph (of Xie Kitchin), and Carroll's own cribbage board, the Burstein association holdings include Dodgson's copy of William Thackeray's *Vanity Fair* with a

♥
Sandor, Martin, and Mark Burstein, 2004
♥

handwritten note; and his copy of Alfred Lord Tennyson's *The Princess*, inscribed with his initials in his own hand, below which is "Miss Thomson, In memoriam: Jan 14, 1898" – a memorial gift to E. Gertrude Thomson from his sister Elizabeth Lucy Dodgson, whose handwriting this is, along with a note from Miss Dodgson to Miss Thomson explaining the gift. Another prized item is a presentation copy of a very large book called *Illustrations of the Bible,* given "to Edith Alice Dodgson from her affectionate Uncle and Godfather."

Mark relates that one day his father happened to be in a bookstore in San Francisco, speaking to the proprietor, when he found his hand unconsciously fondling a book. As the conversation wound down, he noticed that the volume in his hand, *The Holy Land,* was written by the Reverend Canon Duckworth. Duckworth, of course, was the clergyman who accompanied Dodgson and the Liddell girls on a row up the Isis on July 4, 1862, where Alice's tale was first told. The volume is now part of the Burstein Collection.

Pride of place, and of the acquisition dance, belongs to Alice Liddell's flutina, a type of accordion. This dance

♥ Alice Liddell's flutina ♥

was performed by Sandor with several generations of the family who had purchased it in the 1930s from Captain Caryl Hargreaves, Alice's son. It is kept in a glass cabinet that was once used to sell gloves in a department store and now houses the flutina, the cribbage board, a letter from Grace Slick about "White Rabbit," and what Mark – tongue firmly in cheek – calls the "actual" fan, white kid gloves, and "bright brass plate with the name 'W. RABBIT,' engraved upon it" from Wonderland.

Comics and Original Art

Like many others, the Burstein Collection has collections inside collections – such as the holdings of translations of Carroll's works. Comic books have been a passion of Mark's since childhood. As a result, the collection contains what he calls a "treasure chest" of Alice-related comics – about two hundred of them. Some are "very, very rare," like the oversize edition of *Buddy Tucker Meets Alice in Wonderland* (1907), the first appearance of Alice in a "comic book." Mark and fellow collectors Alan Tannenbaum and Byron Sewell produced *Pictures and*

ALICE IN WONDERLAND
10¢
2 STORIES IN COLOR–
Alice in Wonderland,
Through the Looking Glass

ALICE IN WONDERLAND
A Souvenir Tour of Your Wonder Bakery

Alice in Wonderland
meets Santa

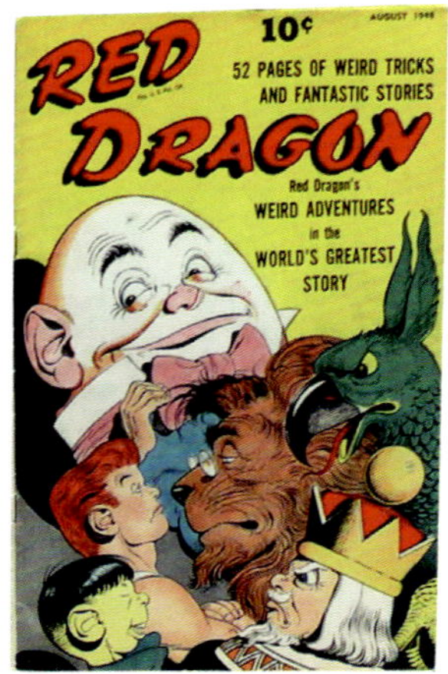
10¢
AUGUST 1948
RED DRAGON
52 PAGES OF WEIRD TRICKS
AND FANTASTIC STORIES
Red Dragon's
WEIRD ADVENTURES
in the
WORLD'S GREATEST
STORY

RAGGEDY ANN + ANDY

TREASURE CHEST OF FUN & FACTS

CLASSICS Illustrated
NO. 49
25¢
FEATURING STORIES BY THE
WORLD'S GREATEST AUTHORS
ALICE
in
WONDERLAND

ECLIPSE COMICS
$2.00
THE DREAMERY

Buffy the vampire slayer
58
SCOTT LOBDELL
FABIAN NICIEZA
CLIFF RICHARDS
EAT ME

DC
BATMAN
DETECTIVE
COMICS

Wonderland
NUMBER ONE $3.50
Disney

Archie
#195
Betty & Veronica
Digest

ARROW COMICS GROUP
WONDERLAND
1

Doğan Kardeş

ALICIA
EN EL
PAIS DE LAS
MARAVILLAS
No. 24
"EN EL MUNDO
DE LA MENTIRA"

MARVEL CLASSICS COMICS
60¢
35
52 FULL PGS NO ADS
ALICE in WONDERLAND
ALL NEW MARVEL CLASSICS COMICS

Conversations: Lewis Carroll in the Comics: An Annotated International Bibliography (Ivory Door, 2005), and Mark collaborated with Craig Yoe in creating *Alice in Comicland* (Yoe! Books/IDW, 2014).

Illustrated editions and original art are another special focus, and the collection includes a large number of original works of art (by definition, each is unique) from illustrated *Alice* editions. They include pieces by Anne Bachelier, Nicole Claveloux, Kim Deitch, David Delamare, Ángel Dominguez, Leila Dowling, Harry Furniss, Evert Geradts, Bill "Zippy" Griffith, Walt "Pogo" Kelly, Peter "Spy vs. Spy" Kuper, Oleg Lipchenko, Iain "Star Wars" McCaig, Dan "Odd Bodkins" O'Neill, Willy Pogany, Byron Sewell, Mahendra Singh, Charles Ware, Wally Wood, and many others, as well as a few signed limited-edition prints by artists who include Ralph Steadman and Iassen Ghiuselev.

♥

A selection of Alice-related comics

♥

A reimagining of *Alice's Adventures in Wonderland* by Mia Araujo

♥

Mark is particularly enamored of illustrations that are at a far remove from Tenniel. An example is a painting by Mia Araujo from the forthcoming *Afia in the Land of Wonders* (Scholastic Books, 2025), which she describes as "a reimagining of *Alice in Wonderland*, inspired by medieval West Africa." Original art of a different nature includes a set of one-of-a-kind papier-mâché sculptures by Edyth Plamondon that Sandor commissioned, a set of hand-painted eggs by Anne Easley, and a unique hand-calligraphed and illustrated *Through the Looking-Glass* by Lawrence Melnick.

Papier-mâché sculptures by Edyth Plamondon

Set of hand-painted eggs by Anne Easley

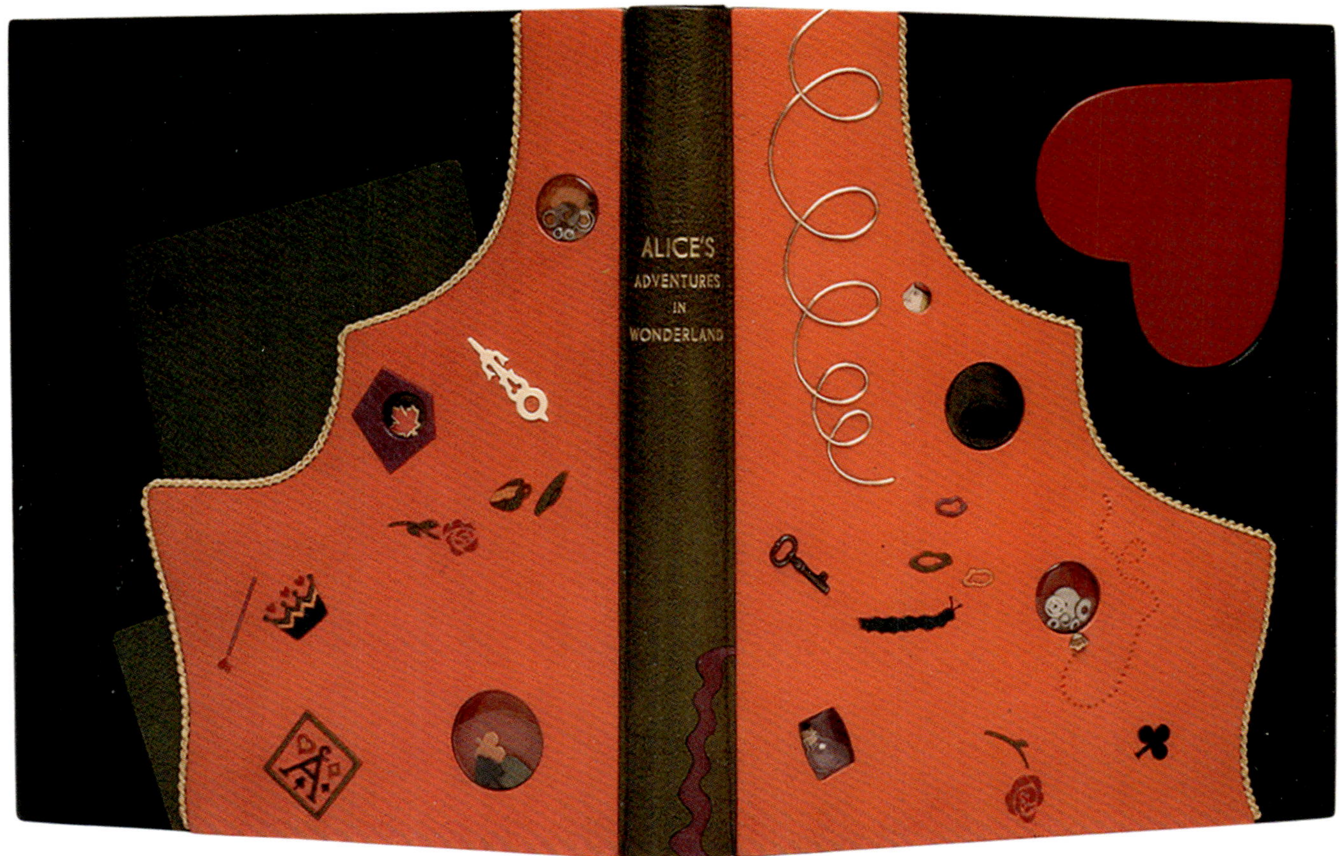

♥

Custom binding by Eleanor Ramsey for the Cheshire Cat limited edition of *Alice's Adventures in Wonderland* (1988)

♥

Infinite Levels

But what Mark loves most is books, books, books of all kinds, shapes, and sizes. In a book collection replete with firsts and association items, Mark notes that the Burstein Collection contains "some lovely editions with fine elaborate bindings," and that "I do particularly love the Cheshire Cat limited editions of the two *Alice* books (1988 and 1998). They were hand-typeset, wonderfully illustrated with woodblocks, printed on handmade paper, and sold unbound. We enlisted the services of one of the world's best fine-binders, Eleanor Ramsey, who made exquisite bindings and boxes for them (many years apart). They are unique treasures."

Mark earned a living for decades in software development, then as a freelance book editor. But through many of those years, starting in 1994, he worked tirelessly as the driving force in turning the LCSNA's eight-page-or-so

Custom binding by Eleanor Ramsey for the Cheshire Cat limited edition of *Through the Looking-Glass* (1998)

Mark Burstein in his Alice room in 2024

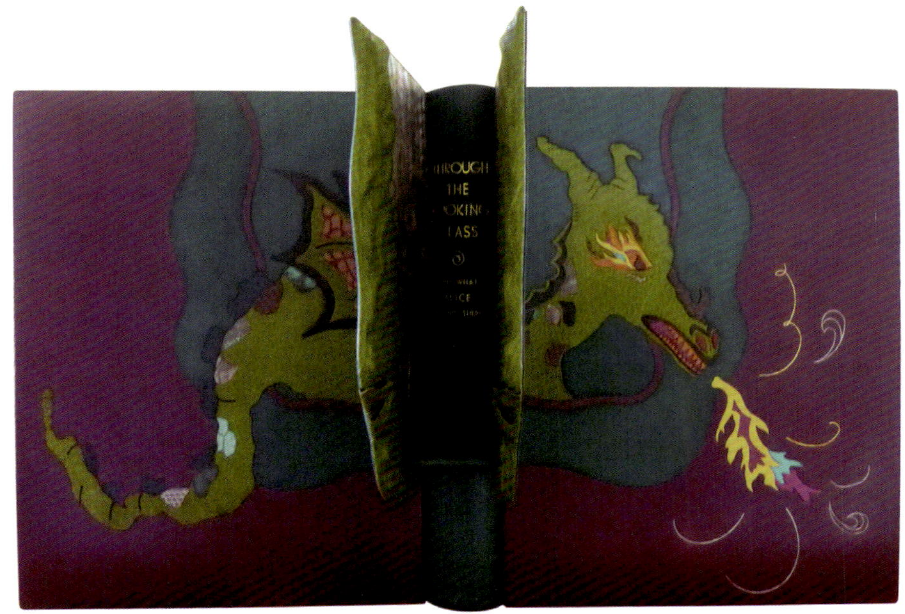

newsletter, *Knight Letter,* into an impressive eighty-page magazine and journal that appears semiannually. In doing so, he certainly saw and learned about more Carroll items, both small and big, than probably anyone. He credits the *Knight Letter* as his "great source of new items" to collect. He relishes the joy of seeing a package in the mailbox "that I have long forgotten was ordered." Plus, there's the triumph of finally acquiring a long-sought item that involved serious, usually global, detective work. Like other Carroll collectors, he deeply appreciates the "camaraderie among the society and with other collectors."

Finally, as a collector and maven, Mark is often asked, Why Lewis Carroll? "Well, first and foremost, the *Alice* books are so wonderfully funny. And like all great humor, that means they are more expressive of the true and deeper ways of the world than that to which the 'serious' can possibly aspire." He notes that in their pages "infinite levels, hidden and secret treasure troves of wisdom and joy, are unveiled upon each new reading, rich in symbolism or suggestion." And, he adds, when people "walk into my *Alice* room, they are usually gobsmacked."

THE
Goodacre
COLLECTION

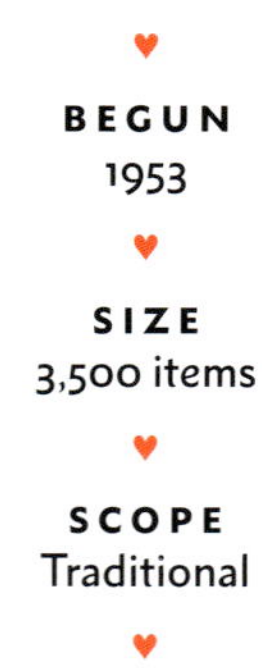

BEGUN
1953

SIZE
3,500 items

SCOPE
Traditional

HIGHLIGHTS
2,000+ editions of the Alice books in English; runs of reprints of the Macmillan editions; 51 original manuscript letters; first-day issue stamp covers

Selwyn Goodacre's earliest memory of the works and life of Lewis Carroll is of his mother reading *Through the Looking-Glass* to him and his three siblings when he was eleven years old. He was, he says, "entranced." His next was when he was thirteen and borrowed Stuart Dodgson Collingwood's 1898 *The Life and Letters of Lewis Carroll* from the library in the town where he attended school. The volume stimulated his interest enough that when he and his classmates were assigned to give a short talk on a Saturday morning on a subject of their choosing, he planned a talk on Carroll. Selwyn, hampered by a stammer as a child, never actually gave that talk, but the perennial Carroll seed was sown.

A year or so later, Selwyn spied an advertisement in the *Times Literary Supplement* (how many teenagers read *TLS*?) offering copies of the paperback catalog of the 1932 Bumpus Lewis Carroll Centenary Exhibition in London for the price of one shilling (worth five pence at the time). He bought it. Perhaps a curious early purchase, but typical of the serendipity of his collecting and collection – though now it goes by the admired term "Selwyndipity."

His clergyman father fed the Carroll-and-books flame flickering within fourteen-year-old Selwyn when he gave him the Derek Hudson illustrated biography of Lewis Carroll upon its publication in 1954. The collection and inspiration, though, are clearly of Selwyn's own making. His father's library had copies of the Macmillan miniature editions of *Alice,* but it was some years before Selwyn even saw the normal-size Macmillan editions. He believes the likely first of thousands of copies of *Alice* that he purchased was a second edition of the Puffin *Through the Looking-Glass.*

Selwyn, a much-admired and now long-retired general physician, was, as a young medical student, "a wee tight" when it came to finances, but on visiting a secondhand book shop he bought a ragged copy of the 6th thousand

1867 edition of *Alice's Adventures in Wonderland*, and a copy of the Sidney Herbert Williams 1924 *A Bibliography of the Writings of Lewis Carroll*. In those days, of course, there were lots of secondhand bookshops. Selwyn began to collect all the copies of the *Alice* books that he could find, and also tried to obtain important journal articles by writing to the magazines and journals to learn if they sold old copies – sometimes with great success, as with the 1932 *Cornhill Magazine* article by the original Alice that he bought for the cover price of the magazine.

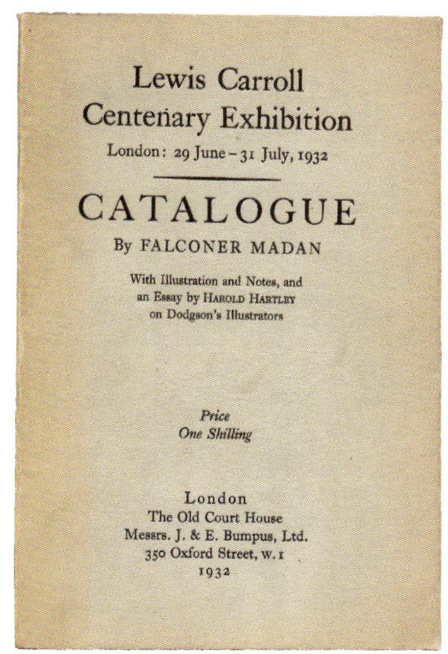

Lewis Carroll
Centenary Exhibition
London: 29 June – 31 July, 1932

CATALOGUE
By FALCONER MADAN

With Illustration and Notes, and
an Essay by HAROLD HARTLEY
on Dodgson's Illustrators

Price
One Shilling

London
The Old Court House
Messrs. J. & E. Bumpus, Ltd.
350 Oxford Street, W. 1
1932

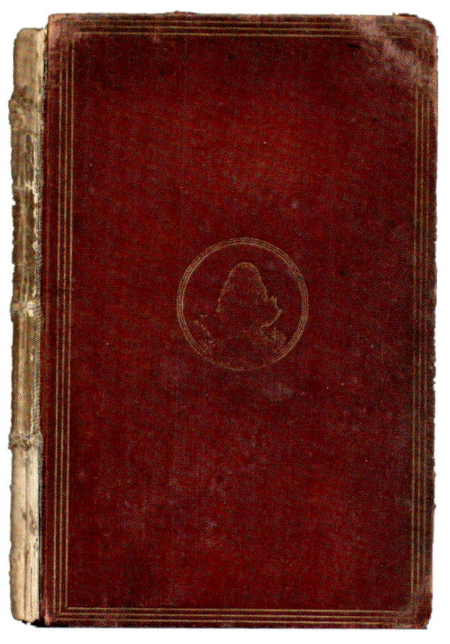

The title page of the catalog for the 1932 Lewis Carroll Centenary Exhibition in London

Selwyn's first purchased copy of *Alice*, an 1867 edition

Two-Thousand-Plus Alices

Once established in general medical practice, Selwyn was able to buy items from a wider variety of bookshops. Later, as bookshops declined in numbers and book fairs became the order of the day, he and his wife, Janet, with their three children (two boys and a girl) would visit towns where book fairs were held on weekends. "Yes," confirms son Mark, "our childhood was marked by lovely weekends when the book fairs were the excuse to get away. But we would have a lovely time." One particular book fair was life-changing for the family. In October 1975 (when Mark was eight), "we went to Portmeirion, in North Wales, for a book fair, and the whole family absolutely fell in love with the village. To this day, we have been to Portmeirion multiple times. My brother, Jonathan, and I became obsessed with the TV series that was filmed there in 1966 and 1967, *The Prisoner*, and we would attend conventions. The larger family went there for my parents' golden wedding anniversary in 2014, and we hope to be there again in 2024."

Book catalogs would also arrive in the post, and for some years Selwyn was able to buy many copies of the *Alice* books, particularly from certain dealers who began to recognize his interests. He, like other major Carroll collectors, cite Justin Schiller, the American dealer of

Selwyn Goodacre in 2023

rare children's books, as being a wonderful source. For example, through Justin Selwyn he was able to buy copies of the very limited editions of the two Morris Parrish catalogues (1928 and 1933), as well as his privately printed "Tour in 1867" (1928).

Selwyn says he has always been quite surprised to find treasures at book fairs that have not been fully recognized by the dealers. One such treasure was a copy of the trial issue of the French Macmillan *Alice* (1869) on offer at a very reasonable price. "This was one of only four known copies," he says. At another fair he found a copy of the rejected 60th thousand of *Looking-Glass* priced at thirty pounds.

"The delight of every book collector," Selwyn notes with a knowing grin, "is when a dealer doesn't know what they have." The Goodacre Collection has been the repeated beneficiary. In the 1970s he visited a rare book dealer in Newcastle, "And he had a copy of the rejected 60th thousand of *Looking-Glass* priced at five pounds. Astonishing! I was so glad to be able to buy it – and it led to my article in *The Book Collector*" about the rejection and illustrated the darker and inferior printing of the 1893 version, Selwyn recalls. "I have three of the known nineteen copies of this edition (according to my census). I have seen notes of a copy recently offered at over one thousand pounds."

Even auction houses may not see what's right before them. One unexpected delight for Selwyn was to buy two copies of later six-shilling *Alice* books at Sotheby's, "Only to find that each one contained copies of *An Easter Greeting* and *Christmas Greetings*, which had been completely missed by the Sotheby cataloguer." Selwyndipity?

A highlight and distinguishing characteristic of the Goodacre Collection began with Selwyn's early enthusiasm to buy every reprint he could of the original Macmillan editions of the *Alice* books, so conveniently printed with the relevant number of thousands on the title pages. To date, for *Alice's Adventures*, the Goodacre Collection contains copies of every thousand from 1866 to 1942, minus about six; that's more than ninety copies. (One cannot be exact, as some issues had two in the same thousand with different dates, and with one or two there is some doubt that they were ever printed.) Although he never managed to obtain an 1865 *Alice*, he did revise Warren Weavers's census of known copies and is glad to have a copy of the 1866 Appleton *Alice*.

Macmillan *Alices*

Of other works by Lewis Carroll, the collection has one of the very few known copies of the Hachette first French edition of *Alice's Adventures in Wonderland*, as well as a prepublication copy. It has copies of almost all editions of *Rhyme? and Reason?* and *The Hunting of the Snark*.

The range of English-language editions of the *Alice* books truly distinguishes the Goodacre Collection and gives Selwyn great delight. He loves the range from cheap "market store" editions costing only pence to grand items like the Salvador Dali *Alice* and the Limited Editions Club *Alice* signed by Alice Hargreaves. On the lower end of the scale, he has several slightly different copies of the Ladybird editions of the 1980s, many kindly given to him by a patient who frequented "car boot" sales.

The Goodacre Collection has similar holdings of *Looking-Glass*. Selwyn himself was involved with the text for the Ralph Steadman edition of *Looking-Glass* (1972), which led to a friendship and a separate Steadman collection. As for the 1969 Dali *Alice*, a mainstay in all major collections, Selwyn says, "I read that only a few copies were arranged to be sold in the U.K., but that if

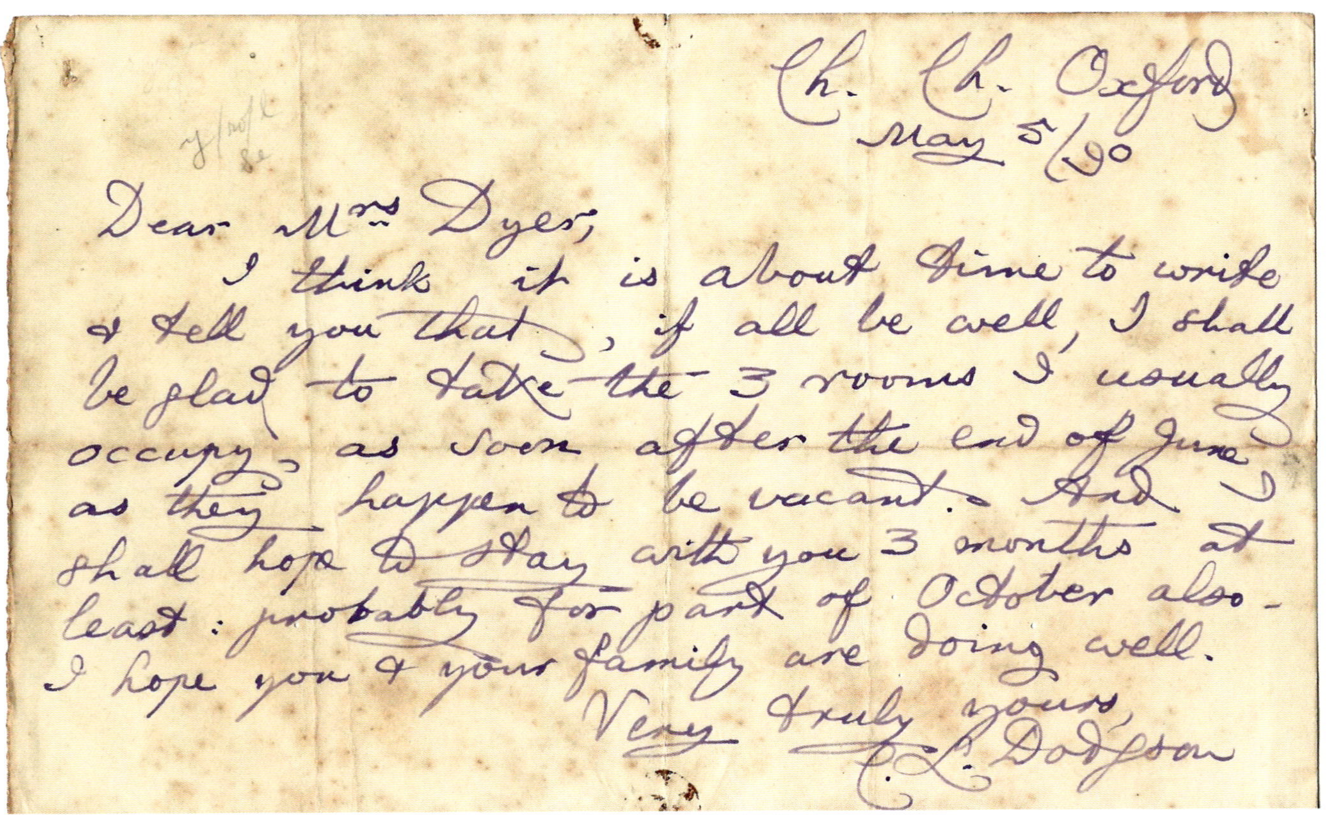

Ch. Ch. Oxford
May 5/90

Dear Mrs Dyer,
I think it is about time to write & tell you that, if all be well, I shall be glad to take the 3 rooms I usually occupy, as soon after the end of June as they happen to be vacant. And I shall hope to stay with you 3 months at least: probably for part of October also. – I hope you & your family are doing well.

Very truly yours,
C. L. Dodgson

♥
Unpublished letter to Mrs. Dyer, asking to lodge for three months in the three rooms "I usually occupy" for the summer in her home in Eastbourne.
♥

I contacted a dealer in Savile Row in London, I might be able to buy one – for around £150. I wrote to them, and the memory of seeing the parcel on my doorstep a while later was a massive thrill."

Letters and Objects

Selwyn regrets he never realized Carroll photographs would one day be of great value, though he did understand that original letters from him would always be of value. The Goodacre Collection now is highly distinguished by fifty-one Charles Lutwidge Dodgson letters, painstakingly acquired over the years. Highlights are five (some unpublished) to Mrs. Dyer, the lady who kept the house where Dodgson stayed in Eastbourne for several summers, and a series of letters to Carroll's child friend Ethel Arnold. Selwyn recounts that when he was a student, he heard that the wife of the Bishop of Ripon (known to Selwyn's father) had inherited some letters

Carroll wrote to Ethel Arnold and had sent them to Sotheby's for sale. He asked her if she would sell them to him at the asking price, and she agreed.

Characteristic of a passionate collector, Selwyn especially prizes objects, such as letters, that touched the hand of his subject. The collection has six books from Carroll's own library, and ten copies he presented and signed. Selwyn laments that acquiring Carroll presentation copies proved "way too expensive!" for a general physician in practice. But his object approach extended to the real Alice as well. He attended the June 2001 sale of material connected with Alice Hargreaves, and was able to buy a 1933 copy of *Alice* signed by her. He already had copies of the 1932 and 1935 Limited Editions Club issues of the two *Alices* signed by her, each of them No. 117.

The bookplate in an 1866 *Alice* owned by her son, Caryl Hargreaves

The Goodacre Collection also boasts a small section of very rare items, such as some mathematical works, separate editions of "Lanrick" and several Oxford pamphlets, editions of the Henry Savile Clarke *Alice* operetta, and copies of all the Carroll biographies, many signed. It also contains one of only four copies of the 1931 *Lewis Carroll Handbook* printed on mould-made paper.

Original pictures are represented by Peter Weevers (his *Alice* was published in 1989) and Graham Baker Smith (his *Alice* was published in 2015). The collection also includes a complete set of the limited edition of *Looking-Glass* and *The Hunting of the Snark* etchings by Ralph Steadman, as well as an original drawing by Steadman (not Alice-related).

Akin to his Steadman collection, Selwyn has another peripheral collection: Harry Furniss (the illustrator of the *Sylvie and Bruno* books), including more than one

Original illustration of Lewis Carroll by W. H. Cattyn that appeared as the frontispiece in the "King's Treasures of Literature" series published by E. P. Dutton in New York and Dent and Sons in London and Toronto in 1930.

hundred autograph letters, as well as an almost complete run of all the other books Furniss was associated with, plus an original picture by him (not *Alice*).

A Touchstone Collection

Over the decades, the Goodacre Collection has been visited by many, and much information has flowed to and from Selwyn. He is a prime connector. There is nary a collector in the world who has not heard him speak on Carroll or exchanged letters or emails with him. He was "almost" a founding member of the Lewis Carroll Society in England in 1969 (he missed only the first meeting), and went on to edit the Society's journal, titled *Jabberwocky* in those days, for years. "*Jabberwocky* was a major feature of our childhood," says Mark Goodacre. "He would collect boxes of the journal every time it was printed, and the kids would help with labels and stamps." Somewhat true to title, the issues appeared regularly but not in synch with the date on the cover.

Through Selwyn's efforts, the world of information about Lewis Carroll expanded. He was an early member of the Lewis Carroll Society of North American (LCSNA), at which he has spoken several times. He first traveled to the United States in 1982 for a meeting of the LCSNA, and met and stayed with David and Maxine Schaefer, who became long-term friends, as have many American Carroll collectors.

Selwyn's scholarly side is often on display in his collection. He has always enjoyed researching topics of interest and has published numerous essays and books. For instance, he investigated the illnesses Carroll suffered, and published an important early essay on his health and medical conditions. He revealed two early Carroll items to be forgeries (*Some Popular Fallacies about Vivisection*, and an issue of "An Easter Greeting" and authorized articles). He is a recognized textual scholar and analyzed the various editions of several of Carroll's works. In addition to listing text changes in the Macmillan editions, he has published two books analyzing the text of the *Alice* books. Selwyn annotated *Elucidating Alice: A Textual Commentary on Alice's Adventures in Wonderland* (Evertype, 2015), with more than six hundred textual notes, accompanied by the original John Tenniel illustrations.

The latest additions to the Goodacre Collection are his own books: *Reflecting Alice: A Textual Analysis of Through the Looking-Glass* (2021) and *Serendipity: The Selected Writings of Selwyn Goodacre* (2022). In recent years,

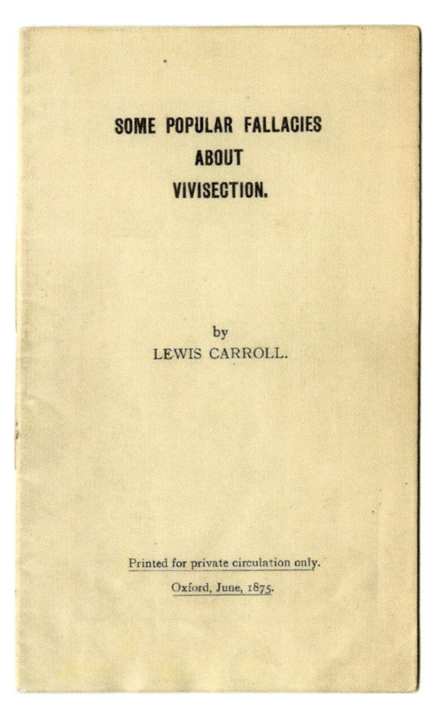
SOME POPULAR FALLACIES
ABOUT
VIVISECTION.

by
LEWIS CARROLL.

Printed for private circulation only.
Oxford, June, 1875.

Cover of the volume Selwyn Goodacre proved was a forgery

Elucidating Alice
A Textual Commentary on
Alice's Adventures in Wonderland
Lewis Carroll
Introduction
and Annotations by
Selwyn Goodacre

Selwyn has also collected first day covers of the 1979 British issue of stamps celebrating the Year of the Child, which featured Alice on one of the four stamps. He now has more than four hundred covers in the collection.

♥

Cover of *Elucidating Alice* (2015)

♥

Hookah-smoking Selwyn Goodacre

♥

The Alice Room

Where to accommodate the more than two thousand copies of *Alice* and a lifetime's worth of Carroll correspondence, journals, offprints, and related items has presented problems. While the children were at home, Selwyn had his "Alice Room" at the top of the house. It was full to overflowing with Carroll books and memorabilia, and there was no room on the floor. He spent lots of time up there, and daughter Nicola remembers hearing the pleasant sound of him tapping away at the typewriter as she went to sleep.

In 2005, he had his garage converted to a Carroll library. But the library is now full to overflowing – a common lament of the great collectors. The Alice Room, returned to its original state as a spare bedroom, is now frequented by his visiting children, grandchildren, and fellow Carrollians.

What will be the ultimate fate of the Goodacre Collection? Selwyn's initial thought was that he would like it to go to the town of Warrington, as it is the closest town to Carroll's birthplace, Daresbury. There are, of course, significant inheritance tax problems involved, and so he is in the process of dealing with a firm of specialist lawyers to help him work through them. The collection may end up selling some of the more valuable items through auction houses – no doubt, to the delight of many eager collectors.

THE
Imholtz
COLLECTION

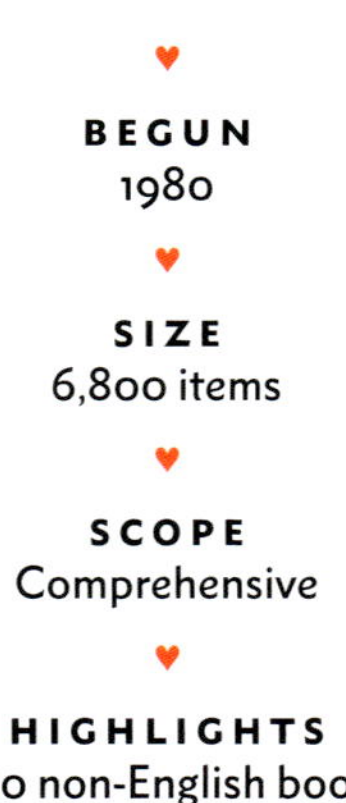

BEGUN
1980

SIZE
6,800 items

SCOPE
Comprehensive

HIGHLIGHTS
1,450 non-English books, letters and presentation copies, original art, yearbooks

In the early 1970s, newlyweds Clare and August Imholtz owned precisely two books by or about Lewis Carroll. Clare remembers reading *Alice's Adventures in Wonderland* for the first time as a sixteen-year-old. Her urtext was a now long lost and forgotten paperback edition. But about six years later, she was given a copy she still has of Martin Gardner's *The Annotated Alice*. Her appreciation grew. The following year, when visiting August's parents in St. Louis, she decided to bring back to their Baltimore home the only Carroll item in August's old library, a thick red-dust-jacketed Spring Books edition of *The Works of Lewis Carroll*. Two books. But the eventual third book, a joint acquisition, made all the difference.

August, who Clare aptly calls her "erudite classicist husband," was, when they met and married, a graduate student in classics at Johns Hopkins University (arrived at via Washington University in St. Louis and the University of Göttingen in Germany). He took from his Johns Hopkins experience a memory of Ronald Knox's Greek translation of "Jabberwocky" and an associated "recreational" interest in studying Latin and Greek versions of "Jabberwocky." Many years later, his after-work recreation resulted in a journal article in the *Rocky Mountain Review of Language and Literature* titled "Latin and Greek Versions of 'Jabberwocky': Exercises in Laughing and Grief." But back in the early 1970s, there was still no *Alice* attraction or collection.

The Imholtzes did "collect" two boys in the 1970s – and a seeming godchild named Alice who lived with them. In other words, by 1989 they lived with seven hundred *Alice* and other Carroll books. The situation led to their boys forming a SAAW society of two: Sons Against *Alice in Wonderland*. They all eventually came to an understanding, and by 2024, the Imholtzes' three-floor townhouse in suburban Maryland (just outside Washington, D.C.) was home to 6,800 Carroll items. The sons moved out to start families of their own.

That third book? A four-dollar used copy of *Lewis Carroll Observed*, which was published in 1976 in association with the newly formed Lewis Carroll Society of North America (LCSNA). At the time, August professed that he and Clare were "only interested in the text," and that it was "the level of scholarship displayed in the book's essays" that attracted him to the LCSNA. The volume contained the address of the society at the time, and in 1978 the Imholtzes became members, as well, of the Lewis Carroll Society in Britain.

That book purchase changed their lives enormously. Early on, the Imholtzes confess they looked upon the "sometimes frantic efforts of the Carroll collectors as a curiosity," says August. That did not last long, as they began to be "intrigued by the various editions, different illustrations, and finally the peculiar pleasure of the collector – the search."

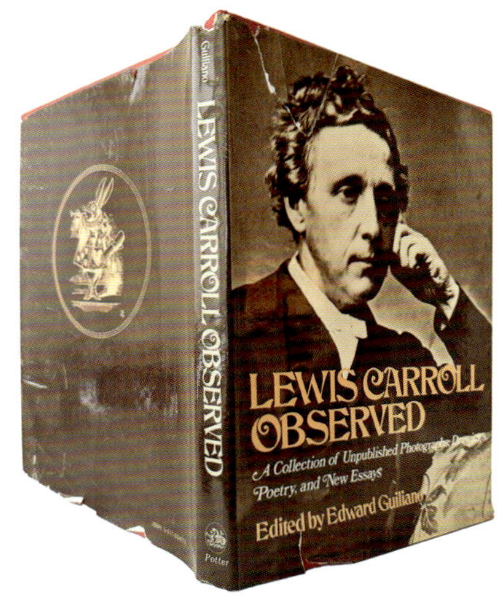

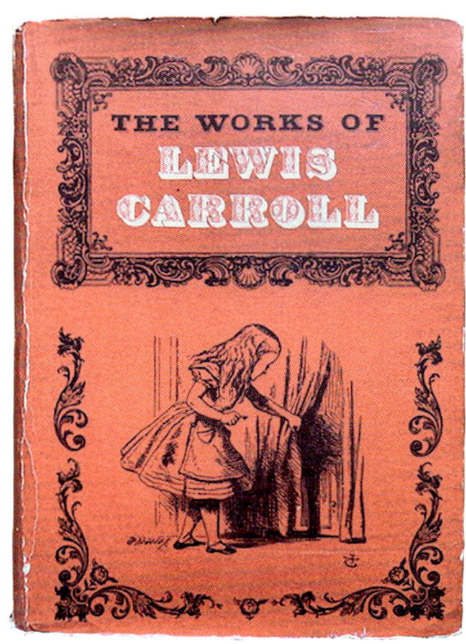

Lewis Carroll Observed: A Collection of Unpublished Photographs, Drawings, Poetry, and New Essays (1976)

The classic Spring Books edition, second impression, 1968

An Extensive and Comprehensive Collection

What is striking about their enormous, comprehensive collection is that as working parents with two growing boys, they were able to acquire it while being "non-jillionaires," to use their term. Both Clare (who has a master's degree in library science) and August held professional editorial and information management positions, and equally impressive is their extraordinary ability as researchers, organizers, and editors, which is everywhere evident in their holdings.

They began their collection in earnest in 1980 by making the rounds of used bookstores and buying on the cheap. Clare recalls once buying fifteen or twenty *Alices* at one shop for about five dollars each and doing serious damage to their budget but having so much fun. Back in the days when anyone could wander the stacks in the Library of Congress, the newly minted collectors

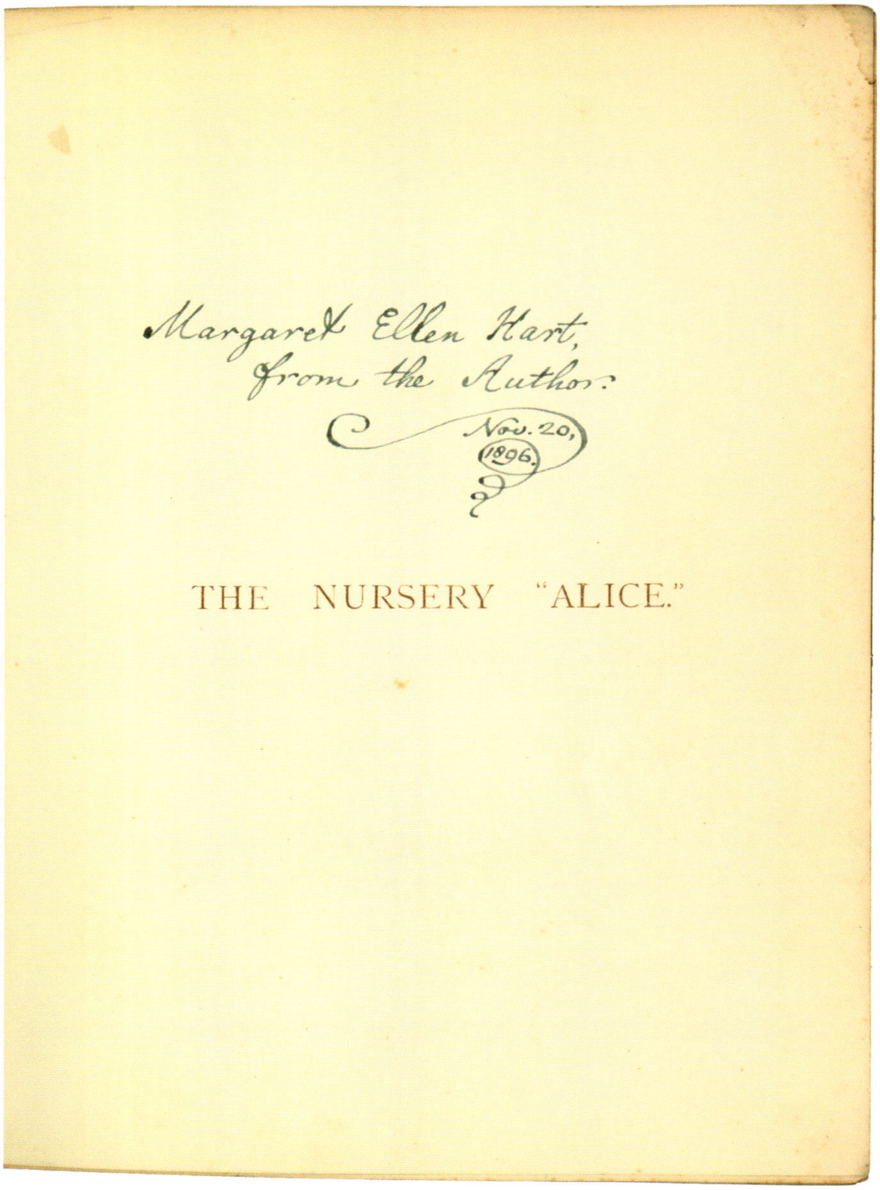

Four-shilling *The Nursery "Alice"* (1890), inscribed by Carroll in 1896

Margaret Ellen Hart,
from the Author.
Nov. 20, 1896.

THE NURSERY "ALICE."

gained encyclopedic knowledge of editions of the *Alices,* then acquired armfuls of their own copies – Grosset & Dunlaps, Hursts, Burts, McLoughlins, Disneys – whatever inexpensive editions they could find at used bookstores.

Then there was a trip to Britain, to the used and antiquarian book capital, Hay-on-Wye. On one lucky day, as they describe it, they found on separate shelves copies of the Mechanics editions of *Sylvie and Bruno* and *Sylvie and Bruno Concluded.* Only a lovingly obsessed Carroll collector would call that a lucky day. One copy set them back five pounds and the other seven pounds.

When eBay entered the collectors' digital terrain, Clare and August acquired a roundel of the 1886 "flimsy" (broadside) by Ellen Whitehead that was used to advertise the first London production of an operetta based on the *Alice* books. They paid less than 4 percent of the previous auction price. "The thing is," Clare explains with a collector's smile and pride, "when you know a thing or two, you will occasionally score lucky finds."

The Rare and Treasured

For any collector of an author, there are special feelings about touching something written by the author in his or her own hand, as well as holding a copy of the very first impression of one of the author's most revered works. With pride of place in the Imholtz Collection are six letters signed by Charles Lutwidge Dodgson in his familiar purple ink. The Imholtzes also treasure their copy of the 1866 Appleton edition of *Alice's Adventures in Wonderland*, which Carrollians know is the first American edition of *Alice*, made from bound pages from the 1865 rejected first printing of *Alice*. It is about as close as one can get to the beginning of the phenomenon we now know as Lewis Carroll and his *Alice*. They also prize a copy of *The Nursery "Alice"* inscribed by Carroll, as well as a number of presentation copies that bring them in direct contact with the purple ink and handwriting of the hand that signed them.

But for such active Carroll collectors as the Imholtzes, the joy and scope of their collecting extends along many avenues. For a few examples: postcards, advertisements, photographs, playbills, theater programs and other theater ephemera, and, of course, illustrations and translations. Meaningful to them among their holdings is the correspondence of a Philadelphia amateur bibliographer, Joseph Jackson, with Sidney Herbert Williams, which was laid in Jackson's copy (copy No. 2) of Williams's

The first Danish edition of *Alice's Adventures in Wonderland* (1875)

A Bibliography of the Writings of Lewis Carroll (1924), plus a drawing of Carroll by Jackson. Another example is a signed photograph of a scene from Hans Richter's 1955 surrealistic Carroll film *8 × 8: A Chess Sonata in 8 Movements*. The cast famously included Jean Cocteau (who was also a director), Marcel Duchamp (it was filmed, in part, on the lawn of Duchamp's summer house in Connecticut), Man Ray, Max Ernst, Alexander Calder, Paul Bowles, Darius Milhaud, Jean Arp, and others.

The Russian Connection

The importance to the Imholtzes of languages and Carroll in the global culture is obvious in a collection that includes 1,450 books that are not in English. You can find among those non-English volumes the first Danish translation of *Alice's Adventures in Wonderland* (1875).

Also among these books are two "favorite" items in the collection: Russian miniature editions published by Kniga of *Alice's Adventures in Wonderland* and *Through the Looking-Glass,* obtained in the hard currency store in Moscow in 1989 and later inscribed by the translator, Nina M. Demurova, and the illustrator, Yuri Vashchenko.

August talks about the life-changing "wonderlandful" experience of traveling to Moscow for business in 1989 and 1990. At the time, he was working for the Congressional Information Service, and was included on a team sent to Moscow to discuss some publishing projects, notably micropublishing some materials too voluminous to reproduce in printed editions. While there, and as a collector always on the prowl, he met with the renowned and ever-so-friendly scholar and translator Demurova.

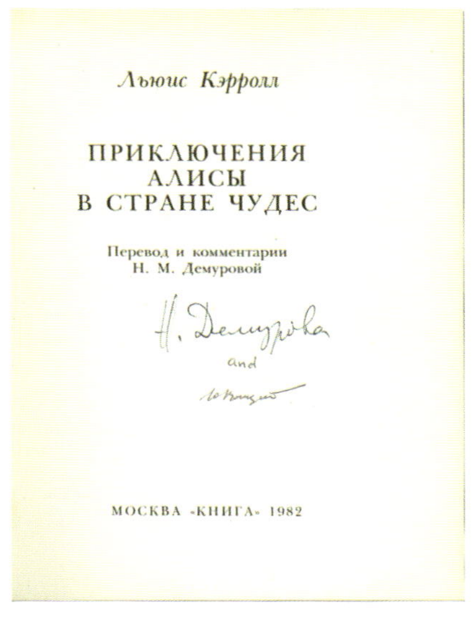

Льюис Кэрролл

ПРИКЛЮЧЕНИЯ
АЛИСЫ
В СТРАНЕ ЧУДЕС

Перевод и комментарии
Н. М. Демуровой

Н. Демурова
and

МОСКВА «КНИГА» 1982

The Kniga edition (1982), inscribed by the translator and the illustrator

1924 Yearbook of Wichita High School, Wichita, Kansas

Alice · in · Wonderland
Edition · of
THE·WICHITAN
Published·by·the·Senior
Class·of·1924·of·the
Wichita·High·School

Printed · by
The·High·School·Press
Wichita · Kansas

She introduced him to the graphic artist Vashchenko, and before August left Moscow Vashchenko gave him a signed print from one of his published *Alice* drawings that was in the Demurova translation.

The Imholtzes' Russian holdings and connections grew much more as a result of August's 1990 return visit to continue the publishing project. Through Demurova, he met the illustrator Oleg Lipchenko, who came by night train from Kiev to have dinner with him. An association via phone and correspondence with the leading Russian Carroll collector, Alexander M. Roushaylo, was also brokered by Demurova. From her, August acquired a set of bibliographic fascicles produced samizdat fashion that contained extensive accounts of Russian translations of the *Alices*. The bibliography was prepared by Vladimir V. Lobanov, a distinguished rare book cataloger at Tomsk State University in Siberia. Over the years, August exchanged "dozens" of books with both Roushaylo and Lobanov, and in the process built up the unparalleled Russian holdings in the Imholtz Collection.

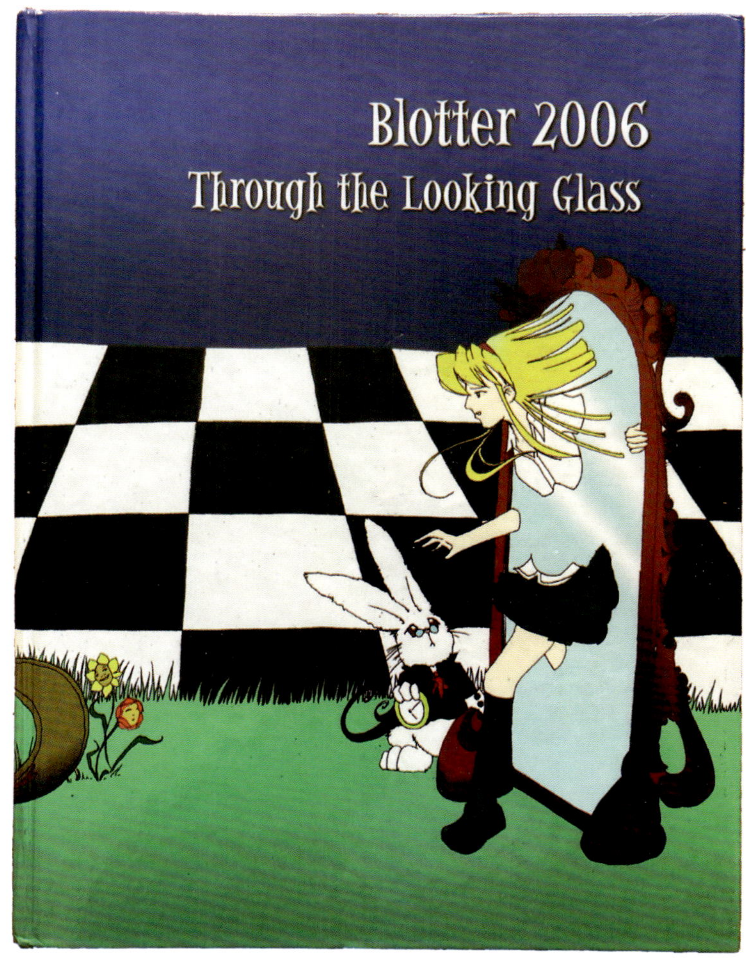

2006 Yearbook of Kew Forest School, Queens, New York

All this stimulated August's desire to learn Russian, which he did, spending "many happy hours at Georgetown University on Saturday mornings." Eventually, during a 1998 return to Moscow, this time accompanied by Clare, he delivered a lecture in Russian under the auspices of the Foreign Language Library in Moscow. During that visit he met Yuri A. Danilov, a translator of some of Carroll's works on logic and mathematics, as well as a young artist, Tania Ianovskaia. Curiouser and curiouser (or maybe not), Ianovskaia eventually emigrated to Canada, as had Lipchenko, and their original Carroll works figure prominently in the Imholtz Collection.

The Yearbook Collection

A surprising niche collecting area that would have been nearly unthinkable in pre-Internet days is *Alice* and/or Carroll-themed high school and college yearbooks. Who knew? Clare started, by luck, to find these on eBay, and

Drawings of August and Clare Imholtz by Oleg Lipchenko (2015)

has now amassed a sizeable subcollection of fifty-five yearbooks, ranging in date from 1924 to 2006. According to Clare, most use student art, often quite brilliant, and several include clever *Alice* pastiches. As an example, the earliest yearbook in the collection, *The Wichitan,* includes pastiches of both Father William and the Lobster Quadrille, as well as student drawings adapting Carrollian scenes to school life.

Friends and Fate

Clare and August and their collection share many similarities with the other collections and collectors in this volume, including these final three parallels. First is that it seems the collector gene, when stimulated, generates both subcollections and often entirely new and different collections. For the Imholtzes, Edward Gorey "is the backup drug."

Second is the joy and pleasures of operating within an affinity group, and many of the collectors in this volume have become long-time friends and supporters. They love sharing their finds and stories with like-minded folks. "We're all mad here," is the reigning value. The Imholtzes especially treasure the friendships they have made around the world, and cite the influence of the LCSNA and relationships with other Carroll collectors for the exposure and stimulation that shaped an important part of their lives and is expressed in their collection. It should be noted that August served a term as president of the LCSNA and Clare served several terms as secretary of the society. Both served at various times on the society's board and on committees.

Clare and August Imholtz, Mexico City, January 2017

Finally, like the compilers of any significant specialized collection, built over time with endless hours of hunting, acquiring, analyzing, cataloging, even writing about it (a special pleasure of the Imholtzes), they face time's winged chariot and the conundrum of the afterlife of their collection. "We would like to see it go to an institution or institutions that could make it available for researchers and enthusiasts."

THE
Lindseth
COLLECTION

The magnificent Lindseth Collection dates to an idea rather than to a childhood experience or an item. Jon Lindseth doesn't remember when, long ago, the idea first resonated with him. But now, as he is about to reach ninety years old, he has lived with it daily for as long as he can remember. It is the idea expressed when Alice asks, "Cheshire Puss…Would you tell me, please, which way I ought to go from here?" The cat replies famously, "That depends a good deal on where you want to get to."

To Jon, a Cornell University–educated mechanical engineer, this is a version of the fork-in-the-road question. In business and in life, one needs to get up in the morning with a purpose and a direction. "It's better to have a plan," he advises. Alice, of course, doesn't "want to go among mad people." "Oh, you ca'n't help that," the sage Cheshire Cat opines, adding one of Carroll's oft-quoted lines: "[W]e're all mad here. I'm mad. You're mad" – introducing a kind of motto adopted by generations of Carrollians. But implicitly most important for Jon is the notion and boldness of following ideas without a final rationale, but with curiosity and respect…and a flexible plan. That has led him to many transformative experiences, ideas, and acquisitions in his life, including more than forty years of robust collecting adventures.

It has also led to a Lewis Carroll collection with one hundred autograph letters written by Carroll and two hundred photographs taken by him. It led Jon to donate some eighty boxes of Carroll ephemera to the New York University Library and 850 copies of illustrated editions of the *Alice* books to Case Western Reserve University. Those are just some atmospherics surrounding the enormous Lindseth Collection.

Jon started collecting as a child. "My father was a stamp collector. I became a stamp collector – U.S. stamps only." He also became nearly self-supporting as an adolescent. He had a paper delivery route at thirteen, and at sixteen was a major distributor of firecrackers – the biggest customer

BEGUN
40+ years ago,
but officially 1998

SIZE
8,000+ items

SCOPE
Completist

HIGHLIGHTS
First and early editions (including, at one time, an 1865 *Alice*) presentation copies, 100 letters, 200 photographs, hundreds of translations

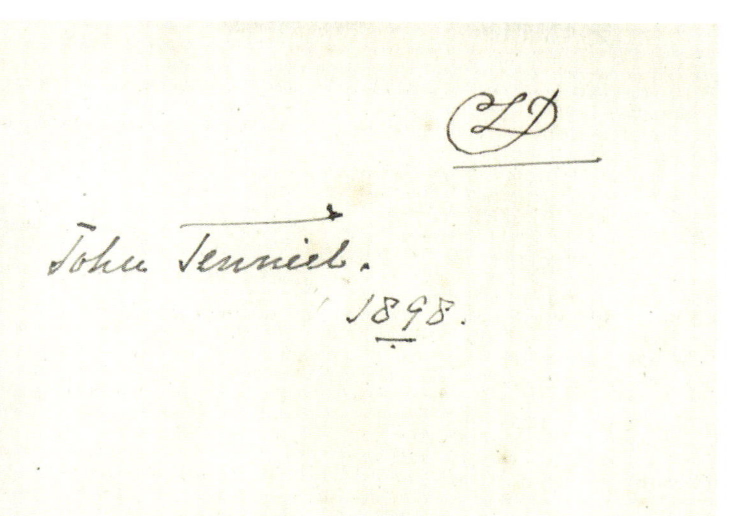

CLD

John Tenniel.
1898.

ALICE'S ADVENTURES
IN WONDERLAND.

Unique copy of *Alice* owned at different times and signed by Lewis Carroll and John Tenniel

of the Allen Fireworks Company of Allen, Georgia, outside the state of Georgia. “I had a lot of money in my pocket when I got to college,” he recalls.

Now living in Ohio, Jon went on to own several companies and brought the electric toothbrush and ear thermometer to market. “It was only when I sold my toothbrush company that I had what I consider an excess amount and started to buy books,” Jon says. He explains, “Real book collectors are buying things they don't need and can't use.”

Л. КАРРОЛЬ
АНЯ ВЪ СТРАНѢ ЧУДЕСЪ
ИЗД ГАМАЮНЪ
БЕРЛИНЪ
1923

With the considerable fortune he made selling his company, Jon started buying Carroll items systematically for his collection. One of his most cherished is a copy of the 1886 facsimile edition of *Alice's Adventures Under Ground* inscribed to Lorina Liddell, Alice's mother. Another favorite is Carroll's copy of the 11th thousand Macmillan *Alice's Adventures in Wonderland* dating from the late 1860s, with a handwritten text change that was later made to the 1869 14th thousand text. What makes this copy extra special to Jon is that illustrator John Tenniel seems to have purchased the copy at the 1898 auction of Carroll's effects; he signed the half title page and dated it, so the page contains Carroll's signed initials and Tenniel's signature.

Jon doesn't know precisely how many items the Lindseth Collection contains. For example, his holdings of Carroll's books in translation, one of his special interests, is exceptionally large. "I have no idea how many *Alice* translations I have. Some time back I even stopped listing them, but it is extensive." Other collectors estimate Jon's "extensive" might mean translations in more than one hundred languages and copies of seven hundred editions.

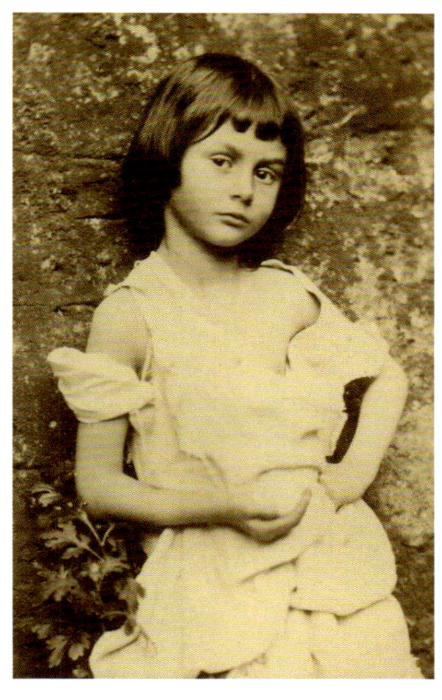

Cover of Vladimir Nabokov's 1923 translation of *Alice* into Russian

Alice as "The Beggar Maid," 1858

A True Collection

Jon did not consider that he had what could be called a Lewis Carroll Collection – not just a bunch of books – until the mid-1990s. One incremental step toward creating a true collection was when he purchased another Carroll collection – as other major collectors have done. He acquired Stephen Rudin's fine collection, which was "strong in letters and photographs," Jon recalls. Then, as a member of the Grolier Club in New York, the preeminent club for book collectors, he provided the first public evidence of what could finally be called the Lindseth Collection. Jon decided to mark the anniversary of Carroll's death with an exhibition there – a sort of black-

yours very sincerely
C. L. Dodgson
(alias "Lewis Carroll".)

AN EXHIBITION FROM

THE

JON A. LINDSETH COLLECTION

OF

C. L. DODGSON AND LEWIS CARROLL

ON VIEW AT

THE GROLIER CLUB

APRIL 1 THROUGH MAY 29, 1998

THE GROLIER CLUB
NEW YORK
1998

tie coming out party as a major Carroll collector. The Carroll exhibition he mounted in the second-floor Members Gallery ran from April 1 through May 29, 1998, with an accompanying 127-page descriptive catalog of the seventy items on display – all but one from Jon's collection.

To Her, whose children's smiles fed the narrator's fancy and were his rich reward: from the Author. Xmas. 1886

Lewis Carroll was an inveterate book inscriber, writing nearly 2,000 inscriptions in his lifetime. The copy shown here is the 1886 facsimile edition of the original *Alice* manuscript written and illustrated by Carroll. It is the precursor of *Alice's Adventures in Wonderland* and is titled *Alice's Adventures Under Ground*. It was originally written in 1864 for Alice herself. Undoubtedly one of the most poignant inscriptions ever written by Carroll was this to Lorina Liddell, the wife of Dean Henry Liddell of Christ Church, and the mother of Alice.

For the 150th anniversary of Carroll's birth, Jon mounted another Carroll exhibition at the Grolier Club in 2015 that focused on *Alice* translations. It was covered by many newspapers and journals, and *The Wall Street Journal* ran a three-quarter-page color story about it. To understand how beloved *Alice* is worldwide, two newspapers in India mentioned the exhibition. Jon was also the general editor, sponsor, and driving force behind the publication of the massive three-volume 2,635-page *Alice in a World of Wonderlands: The Translations of Lewis Carroll's Masterpiece* (Oak Knoll Press, 2015). This magnum opus is filled with authoritative checklists and bibliographical entries, as well as personal and scholarly essays compiled from 252 contributing writers in 174 languages.

Association Copies

With a collection as rich as the one Jon has assembled, it is difficult to point to just a handful of distinguished items, because there are so many. Association copies are one area to spotlight with awe. Association copies once belonged to the author or someone connected with them. Carroll collectors love association items, especially holding something Carroll himself once held. These have pedigree and provenance and stories inside stories.

An unremarkable copy in any condition of *Alice,* say the 1886, 82nd thousand Macmillan edition, would have modest value. However, if it contained a bookplate

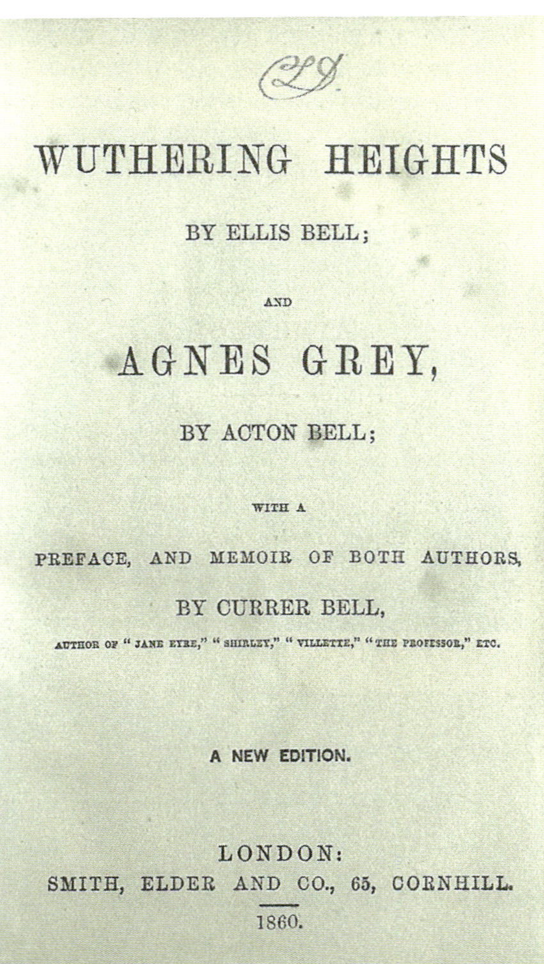

WUTHERING HEIGHTS

BY ELLIS BELL;

AND

AGNES GREY,

BY ACTON BELL;

WITH A

PREFACE, AND MEMOIR OF BOTH AUTHORS,

BY CURRER BELL,

AUTHOR OF "JANE EYRE," "SHIRLEY," "VILLETTE," "THE PROFESSOR," ETC.

A NEW EDITION.

LONDON:
SMITH, ELDER AND CO., 65, CORNHILL.
1860.

Lewis Carroll's copy of *Wuthering Heights*

Title page of the Kitchin-Self-Lindseth 1865 *Alice's Adventures in Wonderland*

or other identifier naming the owner as Véra Beringer (and if you knew she was a young actress in the opening cast of the 1886 Henry Savile Clarke operetta of the *Alice* books), it would be of more interest and value. And if it contained the dedication from Carroll to "Véra from the Author, June 18/88" it would become quite coveted. In fact, this actual volume is one of twelve copies of *Alice's Adventures in Wonderland* in the Lindseth Collection that Carroll signed and gave as gifts to people close to him. Two of them are inscribed copies of the valuable 1866 edition. Both were given to child friends: "To Katie Brine, From the Author" and "To Edith Denman from the Author." There's little question that Carroll items owned by Alice Hargreaves are also especially prized. Not surprising, such association items are among Jon's holdings.

One book from Carroll's library with pride of place in the Lindseth Collection is his initialed copy of the 1860 first edition of *Wuthering Heights.* Jon is also a Brontë collector, so it is no surprise that it is in his collection.

That Jon is a preeminent book collector and bibliographer is widely known. Less well known is that he is also a great outdoorsman, having scaled many of the world's highest mountains and hiked and bicycled all over the world. Undoubtedly the highest mountain in the world of Carroll collecting is the rare "suppressed edition" of the 1865 *Alice's Adventures in Wonderland*, of which only twenty-three copies are known to exist and only six are in private hands. In the world of rare books and collector's prizes, this volume is one of the rarest of prizes. Jon's copy was acquired in 1997 from William Self after years of polite requests by Jon to purchase it, should William ever agree to part with it.

ALICE'S

ADVENTURES IN WONDERLAND.

BY

LEWIS CARROLL.

WITH FORTY-TWO ILLUSTRATIONS

BY

JOHN TENNIEL.

London
MACMILLAN AND CO.
1865.

♥
Xie Kitchin costumed as a Chinese tea merchant (1873)
♥

The copy was owned originally by George William Kitchin, Carroll's Christ Church friend and colleague, but better known in Carrollian circles as the father of one of Carroll's favorite child friends and photographic subjects, Alexandra "Xie" Rhoda Kitchin. She was born in 1864, and later her father gave her the book with 1865 on its title page. She sold it at auction in 1925, and it was one of the nine 1865 *Alices* displayed at the Columbia University Centenary Exhibition in 1932. At that time, it was owned by the Carl H. Pforzheimer Library (which became part of the New York Public Library in 1945). The library sold it to Harriet Borland in 1974, and she sold it to William Self. That 1865 *Alice*, which William did eventually sell to Jon, was on display in his 1998 and 2015 Grolier Club exhibitions.

Nearly "Completist"

Jon calls himself a collecting "completist," but there will never be any such thing as a "complete" Carroll collection; Amazon alone lists more than 10,000 editions of *Alice*. He shares with Edward Wakeling the belief and affliction that "collecting is a disease with no known cure," and it seems "that I set out to confirm it."

In one sense, a large part of Jon's collection is a throwback to the great early and mid-20th century collections of first tier items from Carroll's lifetime. But in another sense – think parodies, translations, illustrated editions, and Carroll ephemera – he is the very model of a contemporary collector.

The only Carroll-related items Jon has never collected is pornographic items related to *Alice*. He was once asked by a distinguished professor emeritus of the Sorbonne, who had done some learned translations in Middle and Old French, "Do you have any Carroll pornography?" "And I said no, but it's a big category," Jon recalls. She said, "With a story about a girl and a hole, you would think it would be." Jon simply said, "Oh boy."

For Jon, the appeal of Carroll is multifaceted, beyond his collecting impulse and the adventure. "First of all," he says, "most people don't realize what a funny book *Alice* is. The brilliance of this guy. Every time I read it, I see something new." He embraces the plurality of Carroll's art and revels in its persistence in the popular culture around the globe.

♥
Jon Lindseth in his office, ca. 2023
♥

A "Cave" for a Collection

The collection currently resides in Jon's notable home in Hunting Valley, Ohio. He commissioned the distinguished architect Robert A. M. Stern to design the house, and it features a library worthy of Jon's rich collections. Jon works from a downstairs office. "My wife calls it the cave," he says. "I've got my computer and all these pictures on the wall. I've got everything you can possibly imagine."

Jon, like many major collectors has built collections within his collection, plus entirely other collections. His Brontë collection, he has been told, is the finest in private hands. There are other very special collections, as well. Jon's friend and Cornell classmate Judith Lowry, of the Argosy Bookshop in Manhattan, persuaded him in 1990 to buy an important book published in 1546 that was the first printed book in Hebrew to ever have illustrations. An example of taking a road less traveled, the purchase led to a worldwide hunt and resultant collection of Hebrew and Yiddish books of fables. Jon also became "the only Gentile who's a member of the Cornell Friends of Jewish Studies." The collection is on loan to the Cornell Library, which in 2023 published the illustrated 546-page *Fables in Jewish Culture: The Jon A. Lindseth Collection*. Always forward-looking, Jon is currently amassing a major Kurt Vonnegut collection. But first and always comes Carroll.

Jon's contributions to the world of *Alice* bibliography expanded in 2023 with his coediting and publishing of a companion work, the two-volume *Alice in a World*

ALICE
In a World of Wonderlands

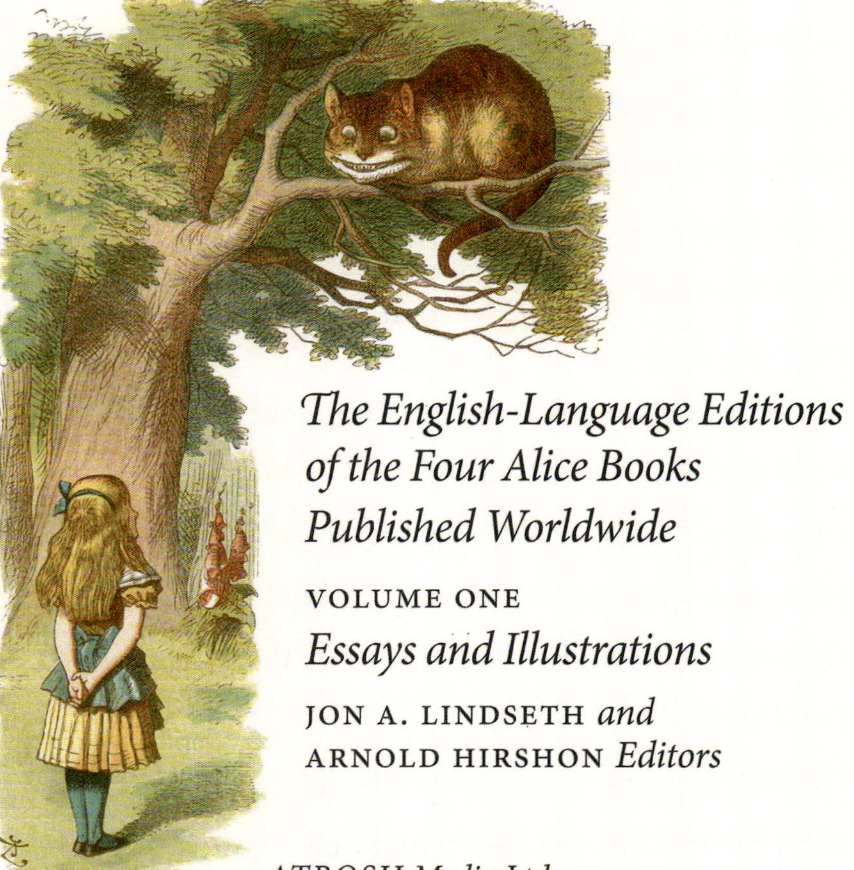

The English-Language Editions of the Four Alice Books Published Worldwide

VOLUME ONE

Essays and Illustrations

JON A. LINDSETH *and*
ARNOLD HIRSHON *Editors*

ATBOSH Media Ltd.
in cooperation with
The Lewis Carroll Society of North America · New York
2023

of Wonderlands: The English-Language Editions of the Four Alice Books Published Worldwide (Atbosh Media, 2023), which includes essays on both the publication and illustration history of the *Alice* books, and checklists of editions published in English from around the world. Jon remains hopeful that some person or group will publish a book on *Alice* parodies.

He no longer collects (except translations), but continues to work with Michael Everson, a linguist, and the book publisher Evertype to produce translations of the *Alice* books in previously untranslated *Alice* languages.

Strategic Donations

When faced with the choice of the eventual resting place for his collection and its 1865 *Alice*, the always forward-looking and planning Jon made some strategic decisions about a decade ago. He had already started to donate items to public institutions. For the portion of the collection he continues to hold, there is a provision in his will to donate the bulk of it to the Oxford University. His reasoning is that since all the major Carroll collections are in the United States, he plans to donate his Carroll collection to Christ Church Library. Underlying the gift is his belief in ensuring that important literary and cultural artifacts will be available to future generations. Such availability will aid scholars in both understanding and appreciating Carroll's creative process and his impact on literature and popular culture.

One item will not go to England, however. Jon decided to put his copy of one of the rare 1865 "suppressed edition" *Alices* up for auction. He did so at Christie's in New York in June 2016, and it eventually was sold to a private American collector for $1.8 million. And so its story continues.

THE Lovett COLLECTION

Charlie Lovett may have been born with the collector gene, inheriting it from his father, an English professor and devout collector of Daniel Defoe's *Robinson Crusoe* (1719). But the gene did not manifest itself in Charlie until adulthood, when he started his serious pursuit of Lewis Carroll – the man, his mind, and his art.

Charlie confesses to a childhood and passing flirtation with collecting stamps, but affirms that when he went off to Davidson College in 1980, he was not yet a collector. Growing up, he knew and liked *Alice's Adventures in Wonderland*, especially a recording of it read by Cyril Ritchard that he wore out playing. He picked up a few copies of Carroll's books while in college, but what he fully embraced there besides a good education was Stephanie Bruck. They married in 1984. On their honeymoon, they decided to become Lewis Carroll collectors.

Today, the Lovett Collection is a formidable throwback to the great collectors and collections of the first half of the 20th century. It has a personality of its own and is distinguished by many objects closely associated with Carroll. But its biggest trophy is a signature item, the rarest of the rare book collector finds, an 1865 *Alice*. It sets the collection apart. But there's more…much more.

Early in the 1980s, Charlie purchased a 1946 two-volume edition of *Alice's Adventures in Wonderland* and *Through the Looking-Glass* with the John Tenniel illustrations colored by Fritz Kredel. It was the first item he bought consciously thinking he might start a book collection. At the time, Charlie fancied the idea of being a single-title collector, like his father. "I knew nothing about Carroll and his other works," he says, "and, at the outset, wasn't even sure I'd also collect *Through the Looking-Glass*."

That notion did not survive Charlie and Stephanie's two-week honeymoon in England in July 1984, where they were overwhelmed by the number of editions available and quickly decided they could not collect *Alice* without *Looking-Glass*. During the trip they happened

♥

BEGUN
1984

♥

SIZE
8,000+ items

♥

SCOPE
Comprehensive without being completist, largely printed materials

♥

HIGHLIGHTS
Materials printed during Carroll's lifetime, books from Carroll's library, translations, theater archive, research library, 1865 *Alice*

♥

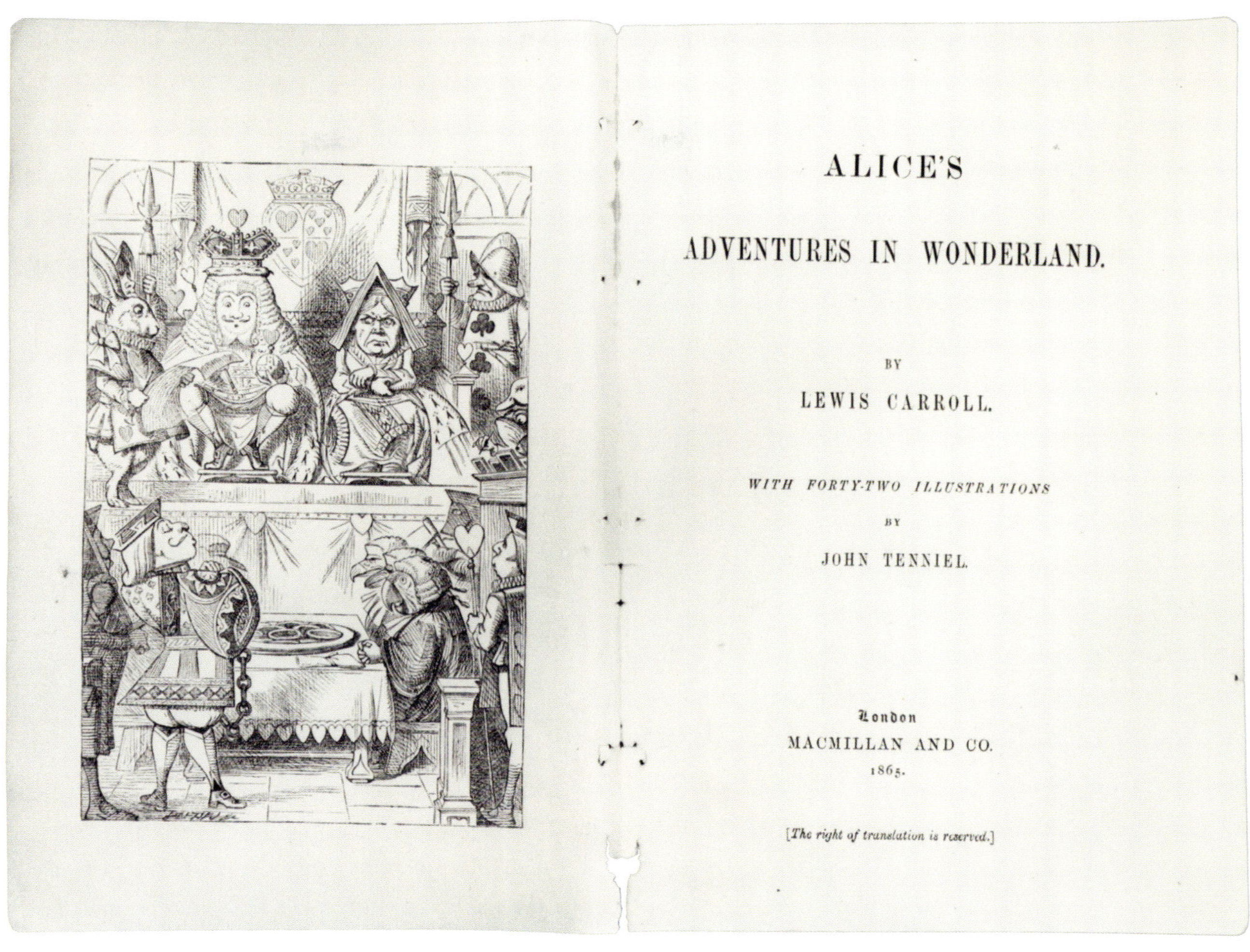

ALICE'S

ADVENTURES IN WONDERLAND.

BY

LEWIS CARROLL.

WITH FORTY-TWO ILLUSTRATIONS

BY

JOHN TENNIEL.

London

MACMILLAN AND CO.

1865.

[*The right of translation is reserved.*]

Charlie Lovett's 1865 *Alice's Adventures in Wonderland*

to wander into Peter Stockham's used bookshop in Cecil Court, London, and asked if he had any *Alices*. Stockham disappeared downstairs and came back with three boxes full. "It was a fish or cut bait moment," Charlie recalls. "We fished." They bought them all. Charlie and Stephanie returned to the United States with eighty editions of the two books.

Other highlights of that first experience collecting *Alices* were finding and acquiring a copy of the Rackham limited edition of *Alice's Adventures in Wonderland* (copy no. 990), discovering there was such a thing as *The Lewis Carroll Handbook*, and that there was a Lewis Carroll Society. The Lovett Collection was officially born.

During their first year of marriage, they made their first visit as book collectors to New York City. Late one day of their multiday buying expedition they found the shop of Justin Schiller and were convinced "we had gone to heaven." They left an hour or so later owners of an Appleton *Alice*, a Macmillan 1866 *Alice*, and a first edition of *Looking-Glass*, plus a few other items. Justin was to prove a good friend to the collectors. It was he who represented them at the auction where they purchased the 1865 *Alice*.

"She went on growing and growing…"

A singular event occurred in 1985 that expanded the collection substantially in size and scope. Seeking out other Carroll collectors from whom to learn, trade, and purchase, the Lovetts pulled names from book acknowledgments and wrote to a few of the collectors. One was Stan Marx, a cofounder and first president of the Lewis Carroll Society of North America (LCSNA), and someone who had collected Carroll for twenty-five years. He wrote back, "Would you like to buy my entire collection?"

Stan was at the point of retiring from a career in advertising. His children and wife did not wish to continue the collection, and the sale would provide a welcome income at his retirement. The fate Stan desired for his collection was that it go whole or in part into the hands of other collectors, preferably intact. The Lovetts visited, discussed, exchanged letters, and eventually returned home to Winston-Salem, North Carolina, from a second visit to the Long Island home of Stan and Diana Marx with forty boxes of books, magazines, and ephemera. The broad-based Marx Collection included nearly two hundred foreign-language editions in nearly fifty languages, several inscription copies, some scarce pamphlets (including the "notorious" *Some Popular Fallacies about Vivisection*), a fine group of parodies, and an outstanding reference library.

Two other Lovett family collections contributed a couple of items that have oversized sentimental value. Charlie's great-aunt was a librarian and book lover with the name – apt for a Carrollian – Caroline Lewis Lovett. When her library was distributed among family members, her copy of *The Annotated Alice* gained pride of place in the Lovett Collection. The other inherited item came from Charlie's father's library, a copy of *Alice* inscribed to him from that same aunt when he was a little boy.

In the late 1980s, Charlie and Stephanie were visiting Justin at his home in Kingston, New York. From there they drove together into New York City for the New York Book Fair opening reception. "We got stuck in a traffic jam and were clearly going to miss the 'rope drop' when eager customers would rush in and snap up all the good books (so we thought)," Charlie recalls. "Justin said, 'Don't worry – if a book is meant to be yours, it will still be there.' A few hours later, we bought a copy of *The Hunting of the Snark* in its original dust jacket. I've never forgotten Justin's words."

Charlie and Stephanie Lovett in their bookstore in the late 1980s

Charlie and Stephanie were so taken with the used and rare book world that in the late 1980s they opened up their own shop in Winston-Salem and became antiquarian book dealers under the name Lovett & Lovett. Charlie has gone on to become an accomplished playwright and novelist. Stephanie went on to earn a PhD and a career in university teaching, particularly religion, philosophy, and writing. Both are past presidents of the LCSNA (Stephanie twice). Both cite the fellowship of other Carroll collectors as a joy of their collecting experience.

By 1990, the Lovett Collection contained approximately 2,200 items, 2,000 of which were meticulously numbered and recorded in a 548-page book: *Lewis Carroll's ALICE: An Annotated Checklist of the Lovett Collection.* Today the size of the collection is somewhat indeterminate, but it is safe to say it contains more than eight thousand objects of all sorts. Charlie has not only stopped counting, but

Carroll's watercolor painting of the Liddell sisters (1862)

no longer sees the value in doing so. "How does an 1865 *Alice* compare to a recent newspaper clipping? Does an archive of Warren Weaver letters and manuscripts count as a single item or hundreds?" he asks. Moreover, in shaping his collection in recent years, especially begun during the COVID lockdown, he has deaccessioned many more items than he has purchased. "I learned that completion is impossible, which is very liberating," he says.

A Working Research Library

The holdings in the Lovett Collection especially point to one trait of collectors: the conscious or unconscious desire to connect in their hands with items that touched the hands of their collected artist or author. The Lovett Collection contains letters, photographs, inscribed presentation copies, and similar, but it is especially distinguished by such items as Carroll's own watercolor painting of Alice, Edith, and Lorina Liddell (1862), and Carroll's early Hammond typewriter (1888), which Charlie had restored.

In the same vein, the Lovett Collection possesses an especially important holding: the largest collection in the world of books from Charles Lutwidge Dodgson's library. As the collection matured in the early 21st century, Charlie came to realize that even if he could snatch up every Carroll item that came up for sale, "I would still never be able to match the completeness of collections like those formed in the past century by Morris Parrish, Harcourt Amory, and Arthur Houghton." He pondered what a collector more than a hundred years after Dodgson's death could provide for scholars. Part of the answer was, to the extent possible, to present a clear picture of the books that Dodgson read and owned, with some insights, or at least speculation, into their influence on him.

Carroll's Hammond typewriter (1888)

Charlie Lovett in his Winston-Salem, North Carolina, home office with Carroll's typewriter behind him on the windowsill (2022)

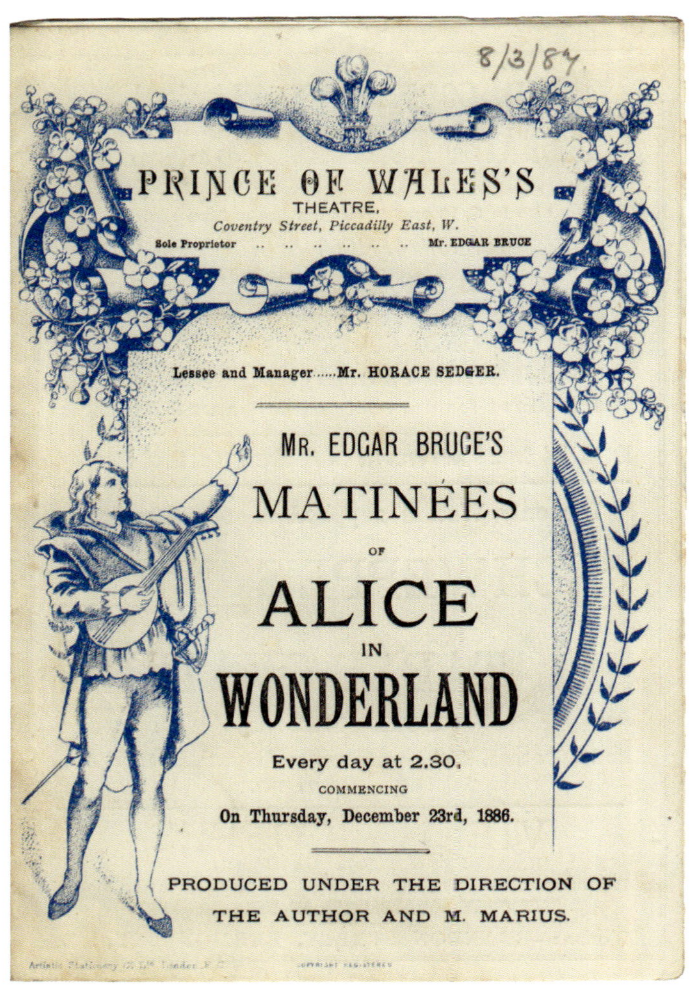

Playbill from the 1886 Henry Savile Clarke *Alice in Wonderland* production in London

Advertising flyer for an *Alice in Wonderland* performance in Bristol 1887

Charlie published his findings as *Lewis Carroll Among His Books: A Descriptive Catalogue of the Private Library of Charles L. Dodgson* (2005). He continues to acquire volumes related Dodgson's library. For instance, the Lovett Collection possesses Dodgson's own set of *Notes and Queries* from its inception in 1850 until his death in 1898. This is more than one hundred volumes (about which Charlie asks rhetorically, "Is this one item or one hundred?").

All this makes for a library of valuable use to Carroll scholars – one of Charlie's goals. The holdings in his collection, similar to yet separate from those in the Wakeling Collection, set those collections apart for their characteristics of a distinguished primary research library. The fate of his collection has yet to be settled, but Charlie says he hopes "it will be useful after I am gone."

The Whole Story

While the Lovett Collection is big, broad, and distinguished as a research collection, it has particular strengths in items printed during Carroll's lifetime, including his own contributions to periodicals, theatrical and performing arts materials, and translations. The collection includes more than sixty of Carroll's rare pamphlets, many in multiple editions, and Carroll contributions to twenty-three different periodicals. It also attempts to set him in a broader context and, as noted, includes many books that he read or owned copies of, photographs of his friends and contemporaries, playbills

PRINCES THEATRE, BRISTOL.

On Monday, May 2, and every Evening during the Week, at 8, and Saturday Afternoon, May 7, at 2.30.

"ALICE IN WONDERLAND."

Written by SAVILE CLARKE.

Music by WALTER SLAUGHTER.

A MUSICAL DREAM-PLAY,

Founded upon the Stories of

MR. LEWIS CARROLL.

With the Original LONDON COMPANY, DRESSES & PROPERTIES.

(MR. EDGAR BRUCE'S COMPANY.)

R.O. HEARSON, PRINTER, 101, LEADENHALL STREET, E.C.

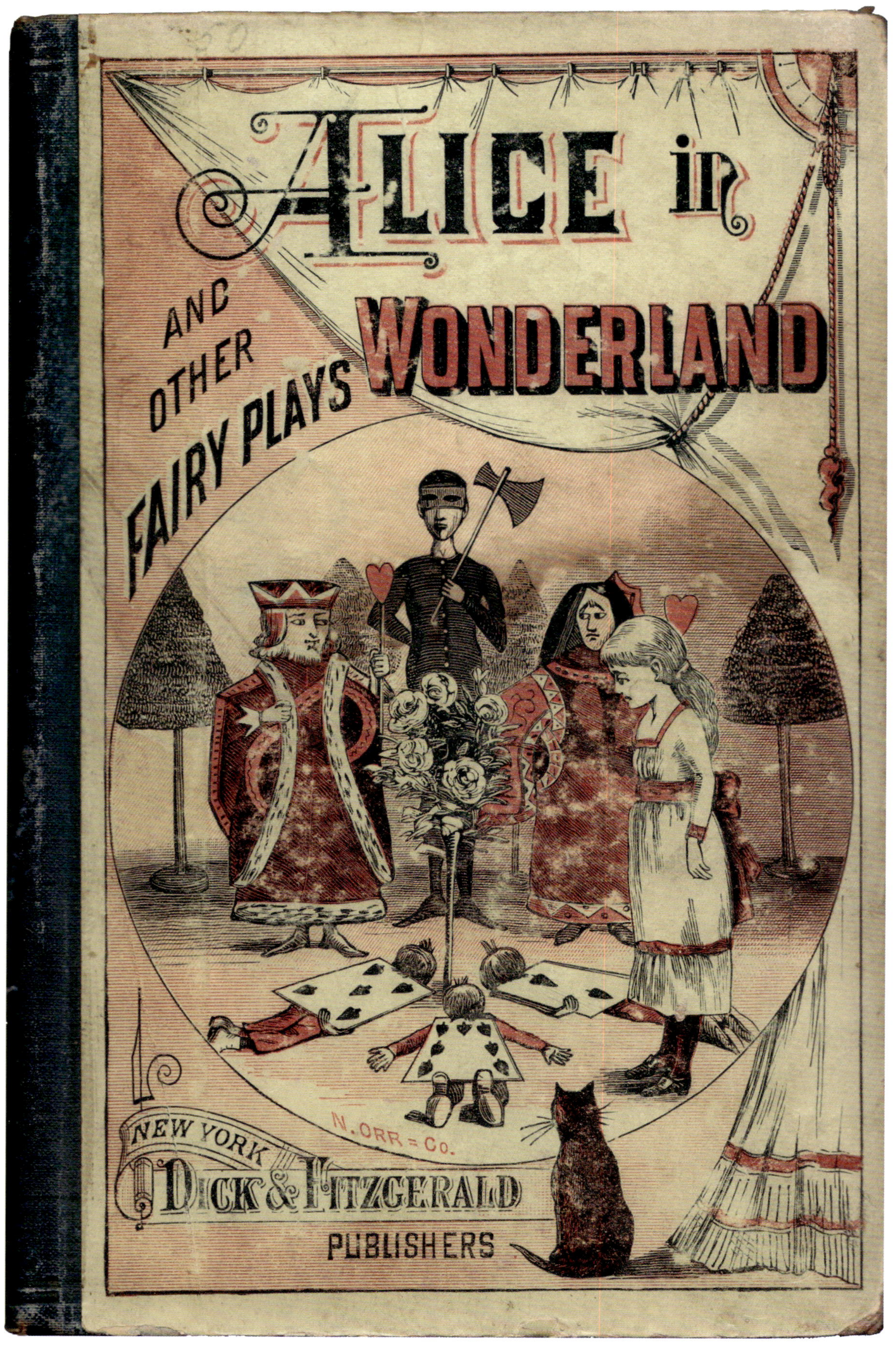
ALICE in
AND OTHER FAIRY PLAYS
WONDERLAND
NEW YORK
N. ORR = Co.
DICK & FITZGERALD
PUBLISHERS

of theatrical productions he attended, books he read as a child, and a wide array of secondary biographical material.

Stephanie provides context and a critical overview: "The information Charlie gathered editing the last Pamphlets volume [Volume 6 of the *Pamphlets of Lewis Carroll,* 2020], and the bibliography, is incredible – hundreds of records of advertisements and reprints, chains of published correspondence, etc. The entire story of Dodgson's letters to *The Eastbourne Chronicle* about vaccination, with both sides reproduced and background information filled in, is not a collectible item, but I would rather have that whole story ferreted out and preserved than own the manuscript copy of one of the letters he sent in."

Although Charlie and Stephanie divorced in 1994, they continue to work closely together on things Carrollian, especially scholarly publications, of which Charlie has made significant contributions, including such books as *Lewis Carroll Formed by Faith* (2022), *The Pamphlets of Lewis Carroll, Volume 6, A Miscellany of Works on 'Alice,' Theater, Religion, Science and More* (2020), and *Charles Lutwidge Dodgson (Lewis Carroll): A Bibliography of Works Published in His Lifetime* (2024).

Illustrated cover of the American edition of *Alice in Wonderland and Other Fairy Plays* (ca. 1880)

Two Theater-Lovers

The superb research library aspect of the Lovett Collection is further reflected in both Lewis Carroll's and playwright Charlie Lovett's love of and in interest the theater. The Lovett Collection of theatrical ephemera is full of rare and unique items – playbills from the 1887 provincial tour of Henry Savile Clarke's *Alice* operetta (with music by Walter Slaughter); photographs of amateur productions from the late 19th and early 20th centuries; original artwork for scenic and costume designs (including for the 1953 London Festival Ballet production); and much more. As Stephanie puts it, "The archive Charlie has assembled of

♥

Cover of Walter Slaughter's sheet music for the Henry Savile Clarke *Alice in Wonderland* (ca. 1911)

♥

programs and photos and other ephemera relating to plays that CLD saw recreates his world in a way that is extremely interesting, and I think more valuable than just focusing on things *by* CLD."

Charlie especially fancies the early printed theatrical ephemera – a "program" from an 1881 performance in Washington Territory, for instance. He points out that things like that, and the papers of Carroll's father, including a Bible, are rare but not necessarily expensive. "I might be the only person who cares about them," he says with a shrug. They illustrate the uniqueness of the collection.

Where is this all kept? In Charlie's specially renovated Winston-Salem home with its office-library extension. There is a six-sheet chromolithographed poster for a 1930s stage production of *Alice* that dominates an entire wall of the office. "I used to visit David Drummond's shop in Cecil Court to sift through old Victorian playbills, looking for shows Dodgson had seen," Charlie relates. Every time I went, David would say, 'I have an *Alice* poster I need to bring you.' He finally brought it out, apologized because he said it was in poor condition, and sold it to me for seventy-five pounds. I sent it to a poster restoration company, who informed me it was in great shape. But it was so large it had to live in a giant poster tube.

"Years later, my second wife, Janice, and I were building an extension on our house, and I realized one wall of my office was tall enough to accommodate the poster. I designed the bookcases on that wall to frame the poster and (other than a stint at Lincoln Center in 2015) it's been hanging there ever since. It's the background to every Zoom meeting I have, and people often ask about it. As far as I know, it's the only one in the world."

The 1865 *Alice* lives in a bank vault. "I bring it out on special occasions," Charlie says, "and especially to share with friends and visitors, from fellow Carrollians to distinguished children's authors of today."

$3,00 Net
R
ALICE in WONDERLAND
A DREAM PLAY for CHILDREN
written by H. SAVILLE CLARKE.
music by
WALTER SLAUGHTER.
W. GEORGE.
ASCHERBERG, HOPWOOD & CREW, LTD
16 MORTIMER STREET, REGENT STREET,
LONDON. W.
SOLE AGENTS:
U.S.A AND CANADA: CHAPPELL-HARMS, INC., 185, MADISON AVENUE, NEW YORK
AUSTRALASIA AND NEW ZEALAND: CHAPPELL & CO. LTD. 250, PITT ST., SYDNEY.
Price 6/- net.

THE Momma COLLECTION

The Momma Collection lives in a bifurcated world. It is partly housed in a dedicated room in Toyama, Japan, where Yoshiyuki Momma and his family live. But that site experienced a version of "No room! No room!" a long time ago. The "There's plenty of room!" solution came in the form of a Lewis Carroll room in Tokyo, where Yoshi works. Toyama is about a one-hour flight from Tokyo.

The Momma Collection, begun a half-century ago, was visited when it was twenty years old by Edward Wakeling, the distinguished Carroll collector and scholar, who recorded his impression of the already "magnificent" holdings:

> It is beautifully organized with marvelous sliding bookcases. Folders, all carefully labelled, contain the ephemera. The range of books is spectacular... an inscribed *AAIW* to Mrs. Dymes, a letter to C. H. Thompson, an inscribed *Vision of the Three T's* to Fausset, a copy of Collingwood given to Gertrude Chataway by Wilfred Dodgson, another copy given to Mary Dorothea Wilcox by her cousin Elizabeth Lucy Dodgson, a copy of the *Picture Book* inscribed by the editor, a photograph of Xie Kitchin, and a letter to Rigaud, a letter to Bosanquet, three Tenniel letters, and so it went on. All highly important and valuable items which made this, without doubt, the most significant collection of Carroll material in Japan....
>
> The range of Japanese editions of *AAIW* and *TTLG* was amazing. I was staggered by the number. Then there were the reference books translated into Japanese: everything from Elizabeth Sewell's nonsense text to John Fisher's cookbook and puzzles. Yoshi also collects Japanese parodies and spin-offs: there are a surprisingly large number of these, too. Japanese writers and poets seem to be very influenced by Carroll.

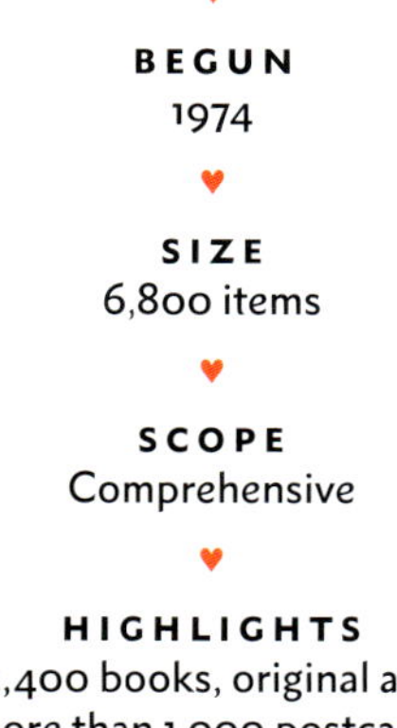

BEGUN
1974

SIZE
6,800 items

SCOPE
Comprehensive

HIGHLIGHTS
5,400 books, original art, more than 1,000 postcards

"No Room! No Room!"
2023 in Toyama

That same year, 1994, Yoshi (president of a company that sells organic fertilizers) became a founding member and the first chairman of the Lewis Carroll Society of Japan. Yoshi's interested in Lewis Carroll dates to 1974, when he was a university student and took a class in *Alice's Adventures in Wonderland*. He was immediately enchanted with it. With the help of Martin Gardner's *The Annotated Alice* and *Bessatsu Gendaishi Techo #2*, 1972 (*Modern Poetry Notebook #2*, special issue of Lewis Carroll, edited by Yasunari Takahashi and Shigeo Kuwabara), he grew "to understand the story deeply" and was consumed by it. These two books hold pride of place in the collection that he began to build at that time. (He confessed to briefly – "gulp" – collecting sake cups, but now only collects Lewis Carroll items.)

Reprints and Friends

In Jimbocho, a district in Tokyo famous for its used book stores and publishing houses, there are about 140 antiquarian and secondhand bookstores. So over the years it was not difficult for Yoshi to find out-of-print *Alice* books, primarily in Japanese. The results mushroomed. The number of reprints is astonishing. The collector and Carroll authority Selwyn Goodacre has remarked on

別冊現代詩手帖第二号
ルイス・キャロル
アリスの不思議な国あるいはノンセンスの迷宮

Bessatsu Gendaishi Techo #2, 1972

A sampling of Japanese reprints

"the enormous number of reprints known in no other language." In fact, Japanese was "a foretaste" of what was to come in other countries and languages.

Yoshi has found it almost impossible to collect every reprint. Even so, he still goes to Jimbocho once a month to try to find Carroll-related books. He says "the most happiest time" for him is to come across a book he does not have. When Yoshi's friends from overseas come to Tokyo, he makes it a rule to take them to Jimbocho to help them find Japanese *Alice* books. Yoshi also takes them to *Alice* restaurants and the *Alice* shop in Tokyo. That list of friends includes collectors Sandor and Mark Burstein, Edward Wakeling, David and Maxine Schaefer, Byron Sewell, and Charlie Lovett, among others. The Schaefers were particularly influential in introducing him to collectors and booksellers in America and England that resulted in many exchanges of books, purchases, visits… and friendships. Yoshi notes, "Collecting *Alice* makes me broaden my views, and I have many Carrollian friends" around the world.

When visiting the Schaefers in Silver Spring, Maryland, in 1980, and viewing their "marvelous" collection, he first saw the Salvador Dali *Alice's Adventures in Wonderland* – at that time the largest *Alice* book in the world. "I was amazed at Dali's illustrations," Yoshi recalls. He hoped

Yoshi Momma in 2023

someday he would add a Dali *Alice* to his collection. That day did not take long to come.

His collection grew with book exchanges with Wakeling and the Bursteins, and Charlie Lovett found him a magic lantern set. Still in the 20th century, when he found "the prices of the books by and about Lewis Carroll were reasonable," Yoshi added to his collection the Appleton *Alice*, the 1866 *Alice*, signed copies, autograph letters, *Alice's Adventures in Wonderland* illustrated by Marie Laurencin, some other first editions of Carroll's works, and, of course, the Dali *Alice*.

From fellow collector and trade partner Joe Brabant in Toronto, Canada, he received the fine press and limited edition of *Alice's Adventures in Wonderland* with ninety-six illustrations by George A. Walker and an introduction by Joseph A. Brabant (The Cheshire Cat Press, 1988). Later on, "Joe was so kind as to send me another book": *Alice's Adventures in Toronto* with an introduction by Brabant and wood engravings and drawings by George A. Walker (The Cheshire Cat Press, 1991). After Joe passed away, Andy Malcolm became Yoshi's prime Canadian contact. Andy and George Walker published a companion volume to the *Alice* that resides in the Momma Collection: *Through the Looking-Glass and What Alice Found There* with ninety-four illustrations by Walker and an introduction by Malcolm (The Cheshire Cat Press, 1998).

Thanks to the late Sandor Burstein, Yoshi added to his collection one of the seventeen copies published of *Much of a Muchness* by Byron Sewell in cooperation with Hilda Bohem and with an introduction by Sandor himself (Chicken Little's Press, 1992).

That led to the start of an unusual exchange program with Byron Sewell, a Carrollian collector and artist of the first rank. For years, Yoshi sent Byron Japanese *Alice* books, and Byron sent Yoshi his works. When Byron came to Japan on business in October 2006, Yoshi took him to the Carrollian places in Tokyo, including Jimbocho. From his experience there, Byron created the story "Makuhari Snark," which was included in *Mishmash* No. 10 (2008) published by the Lewis Carroll Society of Japan.

A Long Quest

The Momma Collection now contains about 5,400 books. That includes the first Japanese *Through the Looking-Glass* (1899), and the first Japanese *Alice's Adventures in Wonderland* (1908). Yoshi believes Japanese is the only language in which *Through the Looking-Glass* was published before *Alice's Adventures in Wonderland.*

For Yoshi, the most meaningful of his books in Japanese is his *Alice's Adventures in Wonderland* signed

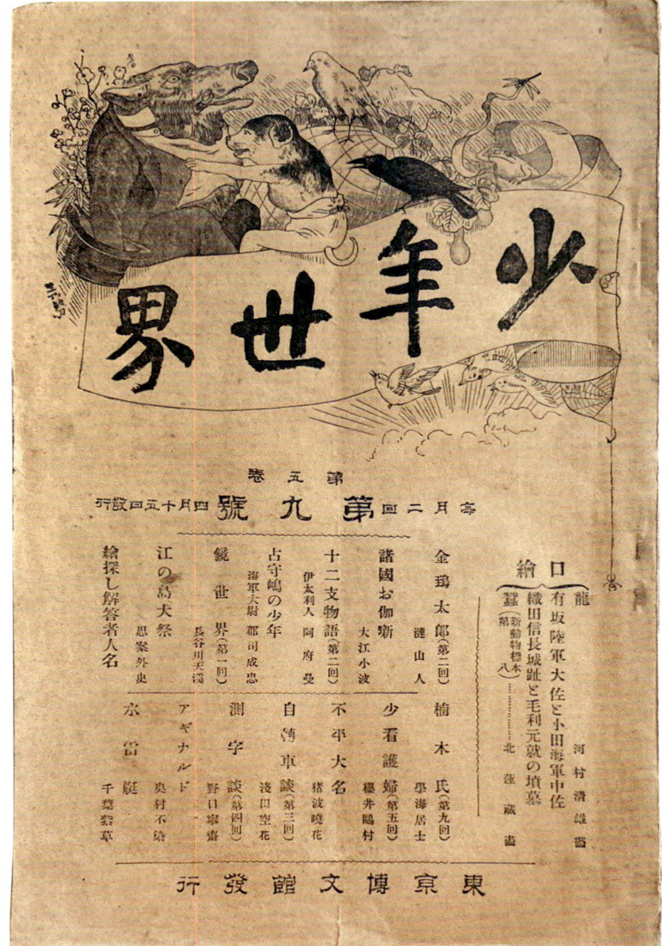

First Japanese *Alice's Adventures in Wonderland*, 1908

First Japanese *Through the Looking-Glass*, 1899

Alice's Adventures in Wonderland pocket edition (shown actual size)

Alice's Adventures in Wonderland published by Seiundo Shoten in 1929, signed by Alice Pleasance Hargreaves

by Alice Pleasance Hargreaves (Seiundo Shoten, 1929, the sixth printing). This book is translated by Aokotori Masumoto and illustrated by Margaret Tarrant. Carroll's child friend Alice had four Japanese translations in her own library, and she signed three of them as Alice Pleasance Hargreaves. The fact she had Japanese *Alice* books in her collection, one of which Yoshi now owns, makes this volume his sentimental favorite. His quest to acquire one of these extremely rare, signed copies was quite challenging. On another long quest, he notes, "In October 2022, I finally found AAIW translated by Masao Kusuyama and illustrated by John Tenniel, frontispiece by Margaret Tarrant (Katei Yomimono Kankokai, 1920) at a book fair in Jimbocho. I had been looking for this book for twenty years."

While it may surprise some to find such a long history of interest in *Alice* in Japan – from reprints to postcards to original artworks, to collections and collectors, to a broad place in the popular culture of Japan – Yoshi points out that as in other countries, "Not only scholars but also

"Alice and the Tiger-Lily" by Shuji Tateishi (2018)

children are fascinated by the *Alice* stories, which are thought of as one of the most popular masterpieces in Japan. So many children . . . sympathize with Alice and her adventures. The word 'Alice' (pronounced *Arisu*) sounds like a Japanese word for young generations. In fact, some babies are named Arisu because their mothers love the *Alice* stories so much."

A distinctive feature of the Momma Collection – and of the presence of Alice in Japan – are the number of miniature editions in the form of both books and figures. Girls dressing as Alice in Wonderland is a popular look in Japan, and is no longer connected directly to the books. The look is reproduced in magazines, advertisements, and

A shelf of miniature figurines

artworks, reinforcing the image. One of the extraordinary original artworks in the Momma Collection is "Alice and The Tiger-Lily," painted by Shuji Tateishi (2018).

Postcards of an Icon

In collections as large as the Momma Collection, it is not unusual to find special subcollections within collections. One such focus is postcards. The Richards Collection in England features a wide range of British images. The Imholtz Collection includes a selection of postcards. Most of the postcards in the Momma Collection are Japanese. The impressive artwork created for the massive number

Postcard by
Maho Mizuno, 2010

Postcard by
Seiko Kusuda, 2015

Postcard by
Yoko Yamamoto, 2008

Postcard by
Takako Hirai, 2018

of *Alice* postcards printed in Japan further attests to Alice as inspiration and cultural icon. Yoshi has been collecting them for a half century, and they were among his first acquisitions. "I find Japanese Alice postcards at the Alice shops, at the Alice exhibitions, at bookstores, at department stores, and so on in Japan. I put them in postcard folders," he says.

As to the fate of those postcards and folders and the rest of the Momma Collection, Yoshi would like to donate it all to a university or museum in Japan after he passes away. He notes that these days some young scholars prefer digital materials to actual books. But for book lovers, the touch and feel of a book is magical and "much more important than digital." When he touches books, Yoshi says he feels "as if books tell me something."

THE Schaefer COLLECTION

The Schaefer Collection is the oldest continuously maintained collection of Lewis Carroll–related books and items to remain in private family hands. Begun in 1892 by Mabel Hutzler (who received an 1891 edition of *Through the Looking-Glass* for her birthday), her collection passed to her son David Schaefer and his wife, Maxine, in 1969, and to their daughter, Ellie Schaefer-Salins, upon David's passing in 2018. Ellie, who lives in Silver Spring, Maryland, continues as a collector-curator of "all things Alice," and has added her mark to the Schaefer Collection as the preeminent collector of Alice teapots.

Her grandmother, Mabel Hutzler, was born in 1884. She read *Alice's Adventures in Wonderland* as a child and told her father, David Hutzler, how much she liked the book. He ran Hutzler's Department Store in Baltimore, Maryland, and traveled to Europe to buy items to sell in the store. On his travels, he bought his daughter any *Wonderland* books he could find, including early translations in French, Spanish, and Italian. Mabel married Solomon Schaefer, and the collection continued growing – first in their home in Colorado Springs, Colorado, and later when they moved to New York City. They had two children, and their son, Ellie's father, David, became interested in the collection as an adult. David and Maxine Schaefer would often add to the book collection when they visited David's parents in New York, even after Mabel died in 1961.

When Solomon Schaefer died in 1969, David and Maxine took over the collection, brought it to their home in Silver Spring, and greatly expanded it. They were both founding members of the Lewis Carroll Society of North America (LCSNA), and Maxine was the secretary of the LCSNA for its first twenty years.

The core collection is full of the old and rare items that were either collected by Mabel or bought by David and Maxine. There are two 1866 editions of *Alice's Adventures in Wonderland*, three Carroll letters, plus first editions in many languages.

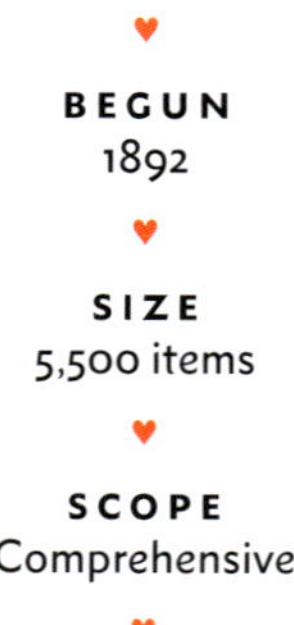

BEGUN
1892

SIZE
5,500 items

SCOPE
Comprehensive

HIGHLIGHTS
Early editions, 100 languages, 16mm films and movie posters, 230 teapots, parodies, miniatures, Alice rag dolls, bathing machine pictures

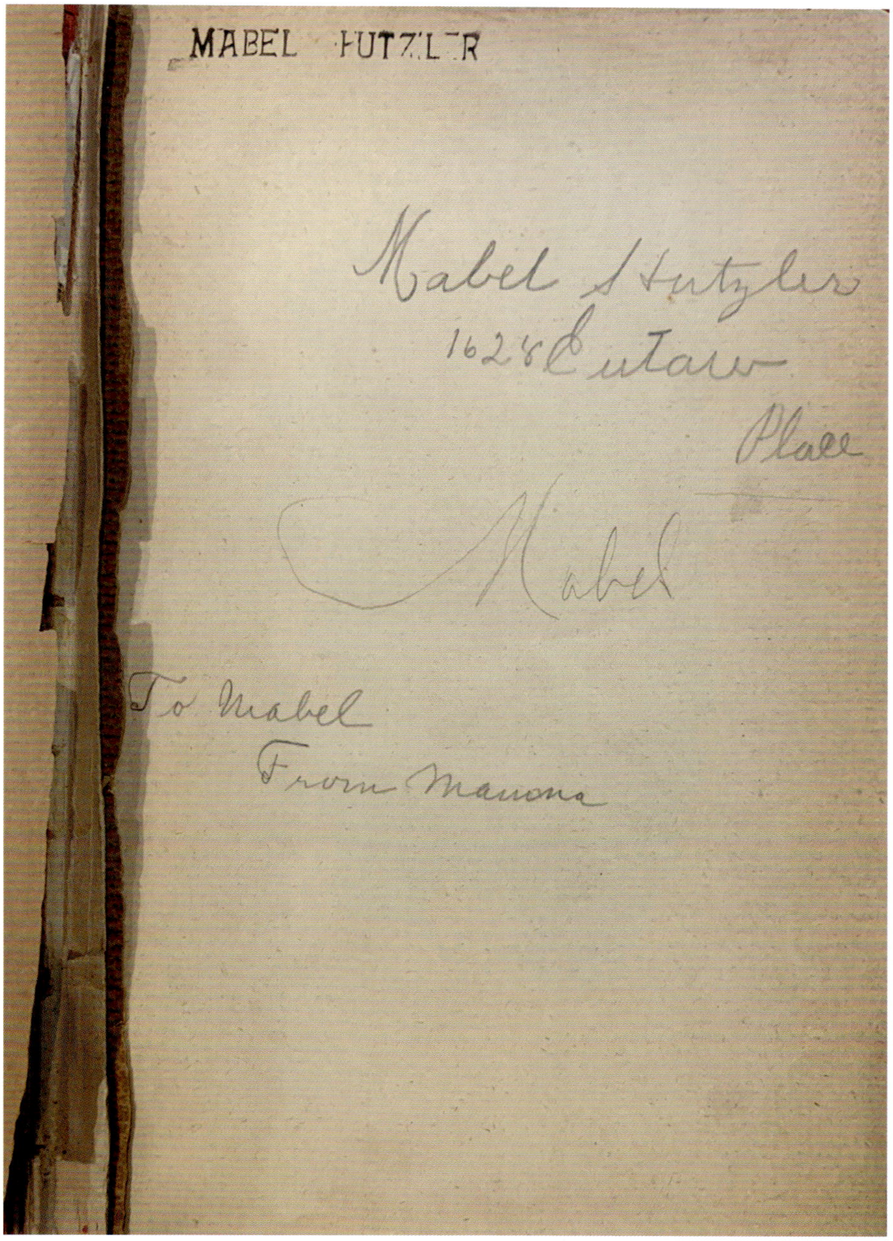

MABEL HUTZLER

Mabel Hutzler
1628 Eutaw
Place

Mabel

To Mabel
From Mamma

The start of the Schaefer Collection, the fly-leaf of the edition of *Through the Looking-Glass* signed and given to her by her mother in 1892

Mabel Hutzler, born in 1884

David and Maxine's home and connection to the LCSNA (of which David served a term as president) became ground zero for Carroll collectors during the last quarter of the 20th century. David was an early computer scientist for the US government, retiring as the head of the computer development section at NASA's Goddard Space Flight Center to become a professor of computer science at George Mason University. Maxine also worked for the US government as an administrative assistant at the National Institutes of Health. Their outgoing nature and generosity

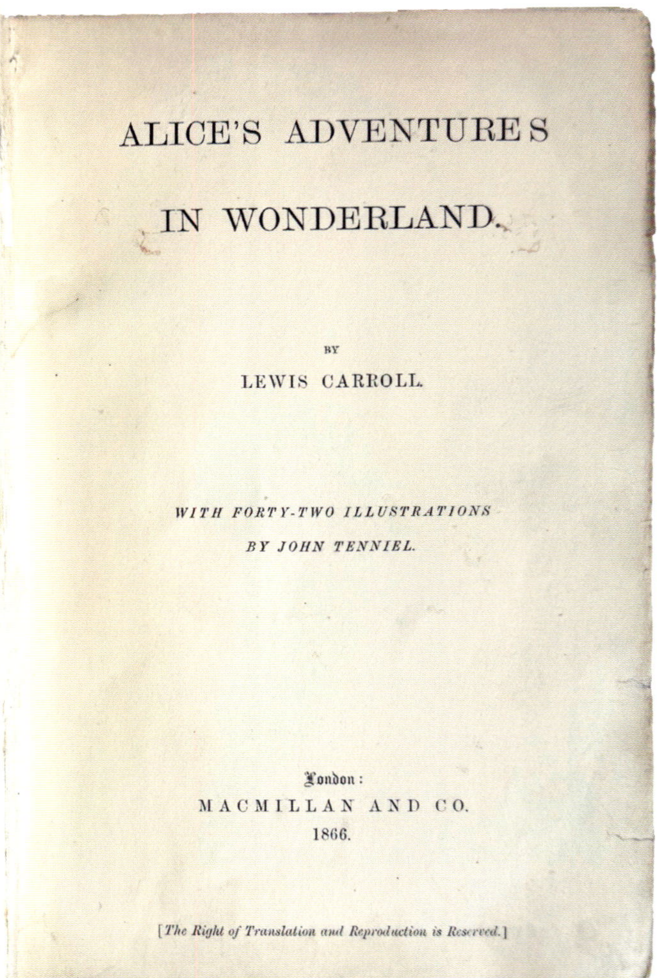

ALICE'S ADVENTURES

IN WONDERLAND.

BY

LEWIS CARROLL.

WITH FORTY-TWO ILLUSTRATIONS

BY JOHN TENNIEL.

London:

MACMILLAN AND CO.

1866.

[*The Right of Translation and Reproduction is Reserved.*]

touched all the major collectors and many others around the world through letters, then emails, along with many personal visits to their home and collection. Most collectors in this volume, from Edward Wakeling to Yoshi Momma to all the Americans and beyond, fondly recount the role the Schaefers played in their lives and the development of their collections.

For Ellie, who grew up with Alice and Lewis Carroll books and artwork all around her, she confesses, "As a teenager and young adult, I hated anything related to Lewis Carroll. It was my parents' passion and not mine." She remembers how her parents regularly hosted Carroll collectors, and she was "voluntold" to help with any society mailings that would go out to LCSNA members.

The Macmillan 1866 first-published edition of *Alice's Adventures in Wonderland*

David and Maxine Schaefer in the 1980s

Ellie Schaefer-Salins in her home, and movie posters for film versions of *Alice in Wonderland*, 2024

The Alice Movie Expert

David and Maxine had a special interest in collecting *Alice* movies. "As a child I had to watch any newly acquired 16mm *Alice* movie," Ellie recalls. "This could be a pleasant or a horrendous experience. Plus we had to pray that our home 16mm projector would work and not destroy the film."

David's fascination with technology and passion for researching and collecting found full expression in his collection of older *Alice* films. He became "the" *Alice* movie expert, publishing the first comprehensive *Alice* film essay and checklist in 1976 ("The Film Collector's Alice: An Essay and Checklist," in *Lewis Carroll Observed,* updated in *The Annotated Alice,* 2015, 150th Anniversary edition). He built on this collecting passion, which he spoke about often, till the end of his life. Indeed, shortly before he died at age ninety-three, David was planning

♥

From the first film version of *Alice in Wonderland* (1903)

♥

From the second film version of *Alice in Wonderland* (1910)

♥

to speak at a film conference in Australia. The Schaefer Collection includes dozens of film adaptations, including the earliest ones, several of which David tracked down and had frames restored, partly by a method he designed. It was David who identified fourteen of the sixteen scenes from the first version of *Alice in Wonderland*, the Hepworth 1903 film version with Mrs. Hepworth playing the Queen, preserved at the British Film Institute. "Even though the film is faded in parts and large amounts of emulsion are missing, it is technically excellent and is enjoyable to watch," he reported. With Maxine Schaefer, who helped him comb the Library of Congress and search old film catalogs with a magnifying glass, David recorded that the Hepworth *Alice* was released in the United States in 1904. Six years later, the Edison Company released their own film version (1910), and it was David and Maxine who traveled to Englewood Cliffs, New Jersey to sort through the Edison holdings for information about the movie and trumpeted its existence. David's intrigue with movies and the technology behind them also led to him proudly acquiring a Lou Bunin Mad Hatter Claymation puppet from the stop-action *Alice in Wonderland* 1948 movie.

Alice in Translation

Books in foreign languages were David and Maxine's other special interest. The collection currently has copies of *Alice* translated into about one hundred languages, including Braille and two different types of shorthand, as well as a range of very early translations, such as the Russian R.I. Rozhdestvenskaya (1909) and Vladimir Nabokov (1923), and extremely rare Japanese and Chinese volumes. The Braille book arrived at the Schaefer house one Christmas day when Ellie was a teenager. "My father had ordered it a few weeks before Christmas and a very nice gentleman wanted to be sure that the blind child the book was ordered for would receive the book by Christmas. We kindly thanked the man and then felt guilty about his special trip to our home that day."

Ellie's favorite translation in the collection is more sentimental than expensive and rare. It is the Māori translation of *Alice's Adventures in Wonderland* that she helped make happen. Her daughter, Lena, attended a semester of college in New Zealand. One of her professors from Waikato University, Tom Roa, worked with Ellie to translate the book into Māori for the *Alice* 150th Anniversary celebration. She then raised several thousand dollars to help print two hundred copies of the Māori *Alice* to give to Māori students in New Zealand.

The Schaefer Collection is further notable for one hundred *Alice* miniature books built up over generations.

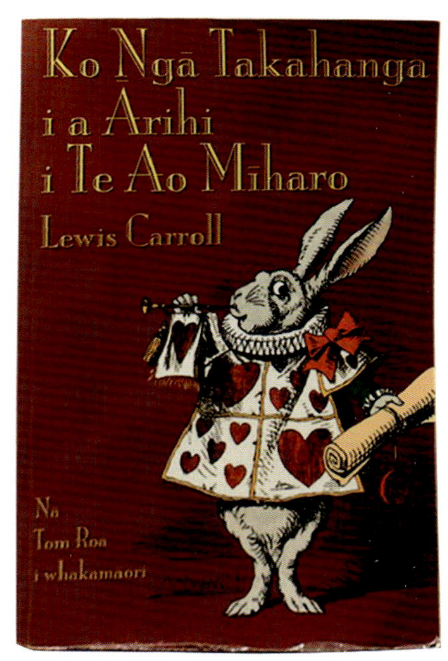

Māori translation of *Alice's Adventures in Wonderland*

It's Always Tea Time

The origin of "the world's largest Carroll/Alice teapot collection" dates to Maxine's sudden passing in 1996. She had started to collect Alice teapots and had eight when she died. At that time, Ellie vowed to continue collecting teapots in her mother's honor. She also began to accompany her father to the biannual LCSNA meetings, where a Schaefer reading of *Alice* to fourth- or fifth-graders

Miniatures in the Schaefer collection

A sampling of teapots

is a tradition started in honor of her mother (and now embraces her father's memory as well).

The teapot collection has now grown to more than 230 teapots, the core acquired in pre-Internet searching and shopping days. The teapots are from all over the world, including England, Japan, Peru, Australia, Russia, and South Korea. It has taken Ellie years to acquire several specific ones.

"Teapots are fun to collect but hard to display," she says. The 230 in the Schaefer Collection are shown in six display cabinets in her home. While she has acquired several expensive teapots that are "works of art," her favorite is the one she designed. As she tells it, "I noticed online that a pottery in England, Carters of Suffolk, had teapots in the shape of books. Each teapot had works by different

INVITATION
Lewis Carroll – Symbolic Logic
Lewis Carroll – Phantasmagoria
Lewis Carroll
Lewis Carroll
Alice's Adventures
In Wonderland
Sylvie and Bruno
Lewis Carroll – The Hunting of the Snark

authors, such as William Shakespeare and Jane Austin, and the character Sherlock Holmes. I worked with the pottery to design a Lewis Carroll teapot with books of *Wonderland*, *Looking-Glass*, *Symbolic Logic,* and more. The teapot lid is an open book of *Alice's Adventures Under Ground* opened to the picture of the cards painting the roses red. (This is to honor my husband, Ken, since he loved playing cards and using cards to perform magic.) I have the first teapot made, and it is now mass produced and advertised in many catalogs. Interesting that people who buy the teapot know nothing of the back story!"

Ellie also collects rag and cloth dolls of *Alice and Wonderland* and salt and pepper shakers, "but not nearly as passionately as the teapots." And she notes that what she inherited and added to was more than objects, and that the best part of collecting is not the hunt or the acquisition, but the Carroll community of friends "that I have met along the way."

When David Schaefer died in 2018, Ellie and her husband, Ken, moved the entire collection to their home, taking everything including the bookcases, books, movies, pictures, plates, comics, parodies, and dolls. Ken had also become interested in Alice and started an Alice playing card collection. He was the treasurer of the LCSNA when he died very unexpectedly in 2020.

Time Will Tell

Ellie, an associate professor of social work at Salisbury University, is worried about the future of the collection when she can no longer care for it. Her children currently

Bookcases in the "oldest" Carroll collection

tell her they are not interested in becoming fourth-generation Carroll collectors. Lena may be interested in the teapots, but not in the books and films. Ellie finds it sad that the collection will not stay in the family, but "time will tell the future of this old and unique Schaefer Carroll Collection."

What will likely stay in the family are the pictures of bathing machines taken in the 1800s that David Schaefer researched and collected with Maxine and his second wife, Mary. As Carrollians know, bathing machines are mentioned in *Wonderland* and *The Hunting of the Snark*. The images adorn a home that he and Maxine bought at Bethany Beach in Delaware that the family still owns.

THE

Tannenbaum

COLLECTION

Collections have rules...and boundaries that determine the nature and scope of the holdings and the strategy and methods for acquisitions and display. The Tannenbaum Collection is distinguished by Alan Tannenbaum's drive to be a "completist and peripheralist." The net result is a collection with probably the broadest range of Lewis Carroll items ever amassed by one person in one place. Very few categories of Carrollian/Alice items are not represented. While the collection is distinguished by its breadth, it certainly is most memorable for having not just one vintage Alice pinball machine but two. Both work, and both are adorned with images of an adult Alice with sensual feminine charms. What a collection!

How best to describe what it means to be a completist and peripheralist? Peripheralist simply means collecting things associated with Carroll or Alice, rather than being by Carroll. For example, letters and drawings by *Alice*'s first professional illustrator, John Tenniel. Or, for that

All printings of all series of Carroll's works, many inscribed, and association copies
Translations, including first and unusual editions of the early translations
Miniature books
Anthologies
Fine press and limited edition books and art
Research library: diaries, bibliographies, biographies, letters
Posters: broadsides, rock concerts, black light, psychedelic
Comic books, including original concept art, proofs, and specials
Original illustration artwork for books and movies
Signed scripts, physical media, vintage and modern
Advertising and ephemera: everything
Music, records: everything
Philatelic and numismatic: everything
Figurines and sets
Books from Charles Lutwidge Dodgson's library
Books from Alice Hargreaves's library
Dodgson's photos
Victorian photography
Dodgson's letters
Parodies and spin-offs
Early and important Illustrated editions: vintage, modern, unusual
Critical analyses
Research library: illustrators, histories of publishing, Macmillan histories
Important auction records
Movie and TV-related memorabilia, films, lobby cards, concept art, cels, props, etc.
Pottery, tableware, collectible plate sets
Stained glass, magic lantern slides
Board games, puzzles, vintage coin-op pinball machines, educational
Statues: indoor and outdoor
Disney
Dolls, puppets, marionettes
Periodicals
Society publications and memorabilia, meeting records and photos

BEGUN
1982

SIZE
9,800 items (+ some tubs of uncataloged ephemera)

SCOPE
Completist and peripheralist

HIGHLIGHTS
First and rare editions, association copies, translations, original artwork, bibliographical oddities, figurines, pinball machines

matter, almost any original Carroll-related artwork in draft or final execution...or movie posters, tea sets, puppets and dolls, and advertisements of all kinds.

Carroll collectors know a peripheral item when they see one. Alan collects them all. As illustration, on the previous page is a list of categories of items contained in the Tannenbaum Collection; those in the first column are categories of "emphasis."

So completist means no boundaries. Alan does admit, "The one area I have cut back on drastically was Disney pins. Pin collecting is big business nowadays, and I simply can't put the time and energy into keeping up with the genre and the unreasonable prices. I am satisfied with the few hundred Alice character and series pins, including proofs, that I already own."

A Moveable Feast...

Back in 1982, Alan was living in Maryland and working as a software engineer and strategist for IBM, a job he held for thirty years before retiring. He was tasked with writing the first commercial spell checker for IBM, and when creating the instruction manual he needed examples of words correctly spelled but not in the dictionary. He thought of the nonsense words in "Jabberwocky," and to check the poem's full text he bought a paperback copy of *The Annotated Alice* because it contained *Through the Looking-Glass.* "I was fascinated by the annotations," Alan recalls. "I had followed Martin Gardner's Mathematical Games for years in *Scientific American* and was first introduced to Carroll in his columns."

That same year, Alan read an article about collectibles, and Carroll (or likely *Alice*) was highlighted. He now can pinpoint the start of his collection to a day soon after when, at the Montgomery Mall in Bethesda, Maryland, he found and purchased a five-dollar copy of *Alice* (Altemus, 1897) and thought he had found an incredibly rare book.

"It isn't worth much more nowadays, but it was the spark," he says.

The Tannenbaum Collection grew rapidly. So did personal computing. "I acquired a very early IBM PC through my job and started to catalog the growing collection from the start" – an invaluable resource he continues to expand.

The "Collector Gene"

Alan confesses to having the "collector gene" big time, as well as being a work-a-holic (a trait he applies to collecting Lewis Carroll and *Alice*). He is fortunate to also have a wife who understands and enjoys the collecting experience. Alison Tannenbaum, a research biologist and herpetologist, has a sizable collection of horticulture books, things relating to alligators and crocodiles, as well as a complete collection of P. G. Wodehouse books (she can recite passages from memory).

"Alison and I would take trips from New York City up through New England, and I was fascinated by antique malls," Alan says. They also developed a joint passion for collecting a few lines of American art pottery, which has its own checklists, cataloging, space challenges, and expertise, along with networking to find the scarcer pieces. But collecting Carroll has shaped their lives. "When I learned of the many editions and printings and bindings, I knew this was up my alley."

In their earlier Carroll collecting years, the Tannenbaums met David and Maxine Schaefer ("their enthusiasm was infectious"), joined the Lewis Carroll Society of North America (LCSNA), and met some members represented in this volume who already had great collections. Alan recalls, "I saw the possibilities and embraced the challenge."

One challenge familiar to all major collectors is where to keep and display their collections. The challenge was

Alan Tannenbaum in his Carroll library (2014)

compounded for the Tannenbaums, as their careers at IBM and the National Institutes of Health took them from Maryland to Florida to Texas to Massachusetts, where they retired. The Tannenbaum Collection moved with them, each move requiring "a significant amount of preparation and handholding," Alan says. "The last move also needed storage of the collection while we built a library attached to our new home for it."

Pinball Machines and a Special Number

Alan was an avid pinballer before college. He recalls, "Many years ago when I learned there were two models of the old electromechanical wood-rail pinball machines with

Alice-themed pinball machines among other objects in the Tannenbaum Collection

a Wonderland theme, I hunted for them. Initially I wanted just the art deco back glass to hang on a wall, mainly because of the floor space the full pinball machines would take." It took him years to find his 1955 Williams (now Bally) in working condition. "We were living in Austin and the collector/seller was in Cambridge, Massachusetts." It took a long time to convince the seller that the pinball machine would have a better life in the Tannenbaum home than in his warehouse. But eventually, "We had it crated and shipped to Austin in time for the 2000 meeting of the Lewis Carroll Society of North America" (of which Alan later became president). "Ironically, five years later we moved to Massachusetts."

On another LCSNA trip to Philadelphia, Alan explains, "We took a side trip to Richmond, Virginia, to meet the owner of the second pinball, a 1948 Gottlieb, the first pinball machine model ever to have electromechanical flippers. He invited us to his attic for his final play with the machine he loved but could no longer store. Both machines have the back glass art I wanted, but they also came with the working machines attached, so when we built our current library, plans included space for both machines.

"Back in the 1940s and 1950s pinball machines were considered gambling and were regulated. I found the little metal license plate an arcade manager had to display to make it legal: Baltimore 1955, and the number was A42."

W. C. Fields life mask

Carrollians will recognize the significance of the number 42, Carroll's favorite and special number. That number has found itself, in no small way, into Alan's collection. "I negotiate for number 42 of limited-edition books and artwork. I add to this when I can, since there is stiff competition for that number among a small number of rabid collectors," he says.

Another of the idiosyncratic holdings in the Tannenbaum Collection that required a patient search-and-seize mission was the plaster life mask made from W. C. Fields's face, taken so that the grotesque vinyl makeup for Humpty Dumpty could be fitted for the 1933 *Alice in Wonderland* movie. Alan had an interest in Fields before he collected Carroll, and when he saw the mask up for auction on eBay it caught his fancy and he aggressively went after it. "When all my bids and offers were turned down," he says, "I contacted the seller. I learned that his grandfather, Wally Westmore, was the makeup artist and costume designer for the vintage Paramount picture, and the mask had stayed in the family. Wally also held the patent for the vinyl masks and costumes used in Hollywood, and the front illustration on the patent depicts Tweedledee and Tweedledum. As it

Views of the Tannebaum *Alice* library room

turns out, Mark Westmore had put the mask on eBay to determine its value, not sure he wanted to sell it. Eleven years later, we struck a deal, and W. C. now rests on a display case in my library."

Appeals to the Heart and Mind

Collectors often have favorite children among their holdings. Some objects hold their special place for sentimental reasons, some for rarity and value, some because they are so exceptional, some for their appeal to the heart and mind. With so many extraordinary items acquired over the past forty-plus years, it is difficult to single out exceptional ones in the Tannenbaum Collection. For Alan, his most recent discoveries give him the most pleasure, but that changes and fades, replaced

by the next things. "I fluctuate depending on which part of the collection I am working on. It might be comics or pottery, rare books or stamps or postcards. Or miniatures or photographs, or..."

For many collectors, the hunt and the find are the most rewarding aspect of their hobby – though contrariwise, nary a collector will deny the primal pleasure of holding items that touched the hands of the author or artist. For Alan, the items in his collection that Dodgson touched – letters, signed presentation copies of his books, and items he owned – are what captures his heart and mind. "I love to open books that Carroll or Alice had in their libraries and flipped the same pages. It is like being with them."

The Tannenbaum Collection contains Dodgson's copy of *Wee Willie Winkie and Other Stories*, and many presentation copies. A few of them are *Alice's Adventures in Wonderland* and *Through the Looking-Glass*, presented

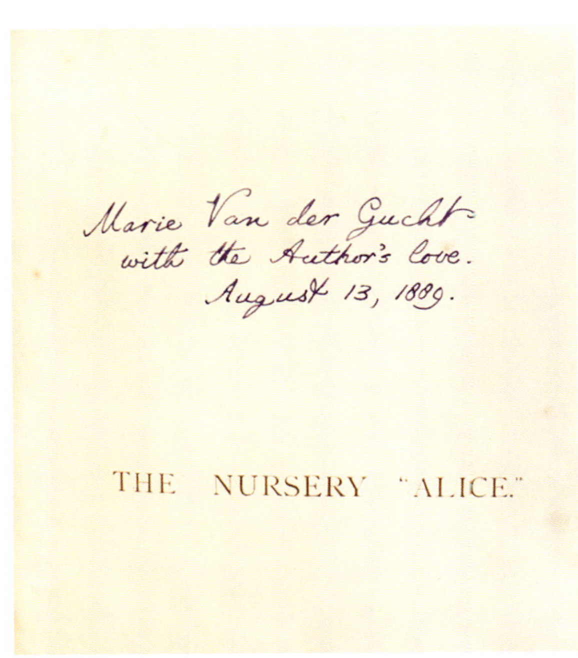

in 1873 to Agnes Elizabeth Sophia Molyneux and her twin, Violet Mary Ann (the performing "Infant Pianistes"); *The Hunting of The Snark* (blue and gold binding) presented to Dodgson's sister Mary; *The Hunting of the Snark* inscribed to Henry Holiday's ten-year-old daughter, Winifred Holiday; *Euclid and His Modern Rivals*, presented to H. A. Barclay; *Phantasmagoria and Other Poems* presented to Alexander Macmillan; and *Sylvie and Bruno* and *Sylvie and Bruno Concluded* presented to Isa Dodgson.

Alan's current favorite is the first of the preproduction copies of *The Nursery "Alice,"* dedicated to Marie Van der Gucht, to whom Carroll wrote the acrostic dedication poem and gave a specially bound inscribed copy. Alan also has a couple of illustrations from that same production run, hand-colored by John Tenniel with Dodgson's approval signature.

It can be difficult separating items with sentimental value from those that are "important." If the house were on fire, Alan would grab his first editions, inscribed books, a few letters and photos – not because they have the most monetary value but because he would "hate to have the Carroll history they contain be lost." He would leave behind – reluctantly – the book with which he feels the most personal connection: that first copy of *The Annotated Alice*, a book Martin Gardner signed for him many years later in Martin's apartment in Norman, Oklahoma.

Social Rewards

Alan is such an active collector that he doesn't spend time developing or ruminating on a useful answer to the question of the fate of the collection. He is happy today caring for and feeding it. He now focuses on online buying, auctions, and reaping the benefits of decades of

♥
Alison and Alan Tannenbaum in Christ Church, Oxford (2013)
♥

networking. Alan adds that the social rewards of knowing others who can appreciate your passion and share in the joy of the hunt is also profound. "The investment value is less of a driver," he says, "but it does help us to rationalize our collecting mania and give us joy."

Alan says he would be pleased to see something good evolve out of all the work and care he and Alison have put into their collection over the years. Actively collecting something of this breadth and depth means that for him, "It is my primary daily activity now that I am retired. I am thankful that I have such an involved hobby. I am never bored, and always find that I am, in fact, behind on projects, and am in daily contact with friends and people that understand me."

THE
Wakeling
COLLECTION

The monumental Wakeling Lewis Carroll Collection – the largest assembled to date by an individual – holds nearly everything Carrollian imaginable, and in substantial quantities, though Carrollians are known to dream up "six impossible things before breakfast."

As Edward liked to tell it, he caught a lifelong, incurable disease at age twenty-nine on Magdalen Street in Cambridge in October 1975. The disease was book collecting, and it was distinguished by an isolated strain of Lewis Carroll obsession. On that date, he purchased for a few shillings a miniature Macmillan edition of *Through the Looking-Glass.*

Sadly, shortly before this essay was completed, Edward Wakeling passed away at age seventy-seven while at his computer in his home in the village of Clifford, Herefordshire, England, on the border with Wales. His health had been deteriorating for several years. Typical of his thoroughness and scholarly (some would say punctilious) nature, he provided extensive information and minute details about his collection right up to the time of his death in October 2023. That includes how an 1865 *Alice* passed through his hands but not into his collection.

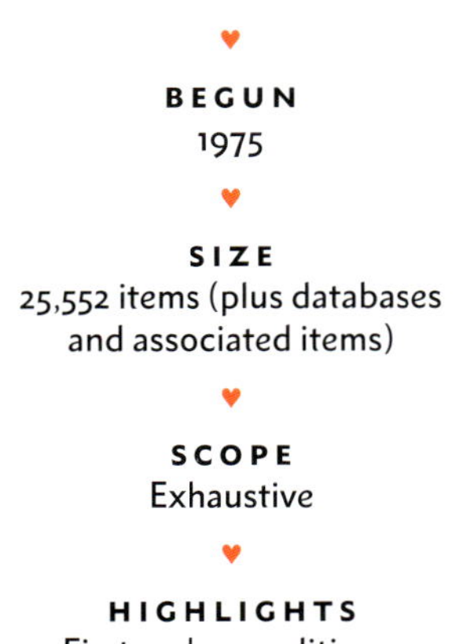
BEGUN
1975

SIZE
25,552 items (plus databases and associated items)

SCOPE
Exhaustive

HIGHLIGHTS
First and rare editions, letters, presentation copies, photographs, translations, reference databases

Begin at the Beginning

Edward's childhood interests tended to logic, puzzles, and a passion for mathematics (not books and literature), and by 1975 when he bought that copy of *Looking-Glass,* he had already been a math teacher for a decade. His father was a "man of the earth," and his mother a homemaker who took care of her brood of six children (Edward was the third child). She read mostly Bible stories to her children. His eighteen-month-older brother did receive a gift of the Heirloom Library Edition of *Alice's Adventures in Wonderland* (1949) with illustrations by Philip Gough. The blue and red cover was Edward's earliest memory of anything Carrollian. He recounts, "In my subconscious mind I suppose the story of *Alice* read to me at the age of four and a half recalled pleasant memories of a happy childhood, and maybe the illustrations by Philip Gough, with their fantastical characters depicted with spindly balletic legs, were in my mind."

According to Edward, "Carroll collectors say that the illustrations you first observe have the greatest lasting impact on you, although you may admire a host of other illustrators that will subsequently cross your path. This is true for me. The memory of the Gough illustrations is still very vivid, now many years on."

Alice finds the White Rabbit's House

Philip Gough's "Alice finds the White Rabbit's House"

University wasn't in his family's vision, but Edward did pass a series of exams that certified him to teach math. During the summer term in 1975, Edward took his school children from Luton, his hometown, to visit Hatfield House, the stately home of Robert Cecil, 1st Earl of Salisbury and chief minister to King James I. There he stumbled upon a Lewis Carroll exhibition set up in the stables (organized by the Lewis Carroll Society). The timing was fortuitous. "I had just completed my part-time degree in mathematics that had occupied me for the previous five years, studied for at the Hatfield Polytechnic," he relates. "In 1975, an intensive period of study was at an end, and I realized that I needed some alternative intellectual stimulus. What I needed was an absorbing new interest." He was able to spend fifteen minutes at the Hatfield House Lewis Carroll Exhibition, but "that was enough. The exhibits revealed a man of many parts, a man of interest and complexity, and a man I wanted to know more about."

Edward continues, "I knew a bit about his mathematics and logic, and I knew the story of *Alice's Adventures in Wonderland*. I didn't know much else about him." Applying to an address in the exhibition catalog, he became a member of the Lewis Carroll Society in October 1975 – the same month he visited Cambridge bookseller Derek Gibbons and purchased his first two red-cloth *Alices*, the 44th thousand *Alice's Adventures in Wonderland* (1874) and the 32nd thousand *Through the Looking-Glass* (1872), for five pounds each. He also bought Alexander Taylor's *The White Knight* (1952) for four and a half pounds. Thus the original 1975 Wakeling Collection consisted of four books. The fact that two of them were copies of *Through the Looking-Glass* confirmed that he was collecting.

The collection grew to eleven books before year's end. The most important book Edward purchased in 1975, however, was a blank notebook. He titled it "Lewis Carroll, Collection of Books, begun October 1975." In that first notebook, for each of the Carroll-related books he owned, he recorded the title, edition, date, place of purchase or dealer's name, and the price paid. It was the beginning of his meticulous Carroll database.

♥
Cover of the Heirloom Library Edition
♥

"A Library of Information"

As Selwyn Goodacre, who saw the Wakeling Collection many times, has noted in what amounts to an understatement, it is "hugely impressive and most beautifully cataloged and arranged." By April 1977, that first notebook was full with 191 entries. By May there were more than two hundred items in the collection, as noted in a second notebook, which ended with number four hundred twenty. The third notebook ended with item number six hundred. By the time Edward completed Notebook 14, there were more than 2,500 books.

In August 1995, Edward converted his card file to a computer database. In 1999, he moved to Microsoft

♥

Bookcases in 2023 in Edward Wakeling's home in Clifford, UK

♥

Excel for his spreadsheets and Microsoft Access for his databases. The Excel spreadsheets gave him the opportunity to go back to the books and record a range of other fields of description: language (for the foreign editions), publisher, publishing details (first edition or otherwise, limited edition, reprint, paperback, and so on), series title, illustrator, translator, whether he acquired the book new or secondhand, date acquired, place purchased and from whom, cost, and other relevant details.

By the end of 2002, the collection had five thousand entries – a milestone he marked by buying an original Charles Lutwidge Dodgson photograph of Mrs. Tom Taylor and her son, Wycliffe. The price was nine hundred pounds. As the collection continued to grow, secondary databases were developed, and an extraordinary research tool emerged for primary and secondary information regarding Carroll's life and works. Edward described his collection as a "library of information." At the time of his death, the database of items in the Wakeling Collection reached 25,552, not counting the ancillary databases and associated information.

It is relevant to note Edward's distinguished role as a Carroll editor and scholar. He edited and annotated the

complete, ten-volume set of *Lewis Carroll's Diaries* (1993–2007), Dodgson's Oxford pamphlets, leaflets, and circulars (1993), and co-edited Dodgson's correspondence with his illustrators (2003). He published a catalogue raisonné of his photographs (2015), wrote a "biography" of Carroll among his close contemporaries (2015), and published many specialized articles and other books.

Edward's meticulous databases are perhaps the most valuable holding in the collection. Some assisted him in collecting, some provided sources for his articles and books, and some are of general interest. For example, they include a complete list, with images (if available), of every known photograph taken by Dodgson; a database of every known letter written and received by Dodgson; and images of any drawings made by Dodgson in his lifetime.

Oxford and Alice

In the early 1980s, Edward decided to continue his education at Oxford University, working on a master's degree in mathematical education and living at Oxford during the 1981 Michaelmas Term until the 1982 Trinity Term. He was attached to Christ Church. Needless to say, he spent a great deal of time there on Carroll research as well as the mathematics he had come to study. He was asked by the librarian at Christ Church, for example, to shelve and value the Liddell/Hargreaves Collection that had been deposited there by Alice's granddaughter. In 1985, with his master's degree in hand, he left the post of head of mathematics at Stopsley High School (where he had been for eighteen years) and joined the Bedfordshire Education Service as a school adviser.

During this period, Edward not only expanded his network of families associated with Lewis Carroll and further secured his special relationship with the Dodgson heirs and estate, but also worked with auction houses and dealers to build up his databases of information about Carroll's life and works.

The Davis Collection

Through the Lewis Carroll Society, Edward met and became good friends with John Davis and his family. John was the chairman of the Society when Edward joined, as well as one of the organizers of the 1975 Hatfield House exhibition. (Edward later served as secretary and some years later chairman of the Society.) John began his Carroll collection in 1948 at the age of seventeen, and by the time he reached fifty it had grown to 4,500 items, one of which was a suppressed copy of the 1865 *Alice*. John was serving a second term as chairman in 1981 when he died suddenly. Shortly thereafter, John's wife, June, asked Edward to catalog and value the Davis Collection so it could be transferred as part of his estate to his two children. Edward completed the task in February 1985. Two years later, in May 1987, June and her children invited Edward to their home and told him they had decided to sell the collection.

Before he arrived (unknown to Edward), they had called the Carroll collector and antiquarian book dealer Jeffrey Stern to assess the collection, which he determined had seventeen or eighteen key items, plus the 1865 *Alice*, but said the remaining items would not be of interest to an auction house. Minus the 1865 *Alice*, the collection's worth totaled about £25,000 – a sum Edward agreed with. That day, on the forty-minute drive home to Luton from the Davis home, Edward came up with the idea of buying the entire collection except for the 1865 *Alice* and worked out what he could afford. When he arrived home he wrote a letter to June offering to purchase the collection at its appraised price, except he would need to defer some payments over the next three years. She agreed, and Edward remortgaged his townhouse to raise money for the purchase. June eventually elected to keep the Salvador Dali *Alice* and a few prints and other items, so Edward ended up paying £21,500.

Unique extant Charles Lutwidge Dodgson photograph of Rances Menella "Neela" Wilcox and Mary "Molly" Beatrice Evans (1876)

In February 1988 the transfer began, and the Wakeling Collection quadrupled in size. And the 1865 *Alice* that Edward could not afford and that John Davis purchased for less than one thousand pounds? It was now appraised at £80,000. Jeffrey Stern purchased it as its fair price, and, working with the New York dealer Justin Schiller, sold it, according to Edward, for about £150,000 to an American collector.

When Edward was forty-two years old, his local government salary gave him the opportunity (with the help of another mortgage) to purchase a little cottage at Clifford, just three and a half miles from the book town of Hay-on-Wye, which would become his permanent home when he retired, and home of the Wakeling Collection.

The change also provided him with increased opportunity to travel, and traveling meant places with secondhand bookshops, both domestically and internationally. The collection grew steadily, as did his contacts with collectors around the world. The richness of translations in the Wakeling Collection is just one piece of evidence. It holds, for example, more than three hundred Japanese *Alices,* thanks in part to fellow collector Yoshiyuki "Yoshi" Momma.

Carroll Photographs

Edward made his first trip to the United States in 1982, staying with collectors David and Maxine Schaefer, as he did on repeat visits. Those visits took him to all the large public and private collections, including month-long stays at both Princeton University and the University of Texas at Austin to research Carroll's photographs.

The Wakeling Collection boasts more than thirty photographs, and many others passed through Edward's hands to other collectors. In November 1988 he purchased his first original photograph, a carte-de-visite of Alexandra "Xie" Kitchin, taken by Carroll on July 17, 1878.

A Full-Time Collector

In 1999, Edward became, in effect, a full-time Carroll collector and chronicler. As Edward tells it, in June 1999, he and all his work colleagues at the Bedfordshire Education Department were ushered into a hall, and "it was announced that we were all redundant. However, we could reapply for our jobs, but only half of the positions would be available. The rest were encouraged to take voluntary redundancy or move elsewhere. I guess I was the only person present who was inwardly smiling." He applied for early retirement, and it was granted in August 1999. Not only did this trigger his pension, but his employers extended the length of his service by three years to increase his pension, paid him a lump sum, and also gave him a considerable amount in severance pay.

The net result was he engaged a contractor to expand and renovate his cottage to create a home in which his Carroll collection was the prime driver of design. This included raising the roof three feet, creating rooms for a research library, a "paper room," and shelves for 150 boxes of books – which, with the help of friends, were moved in one day in December 1999 when the cottage renovations were done. He never again lived in his Luton townhouse.

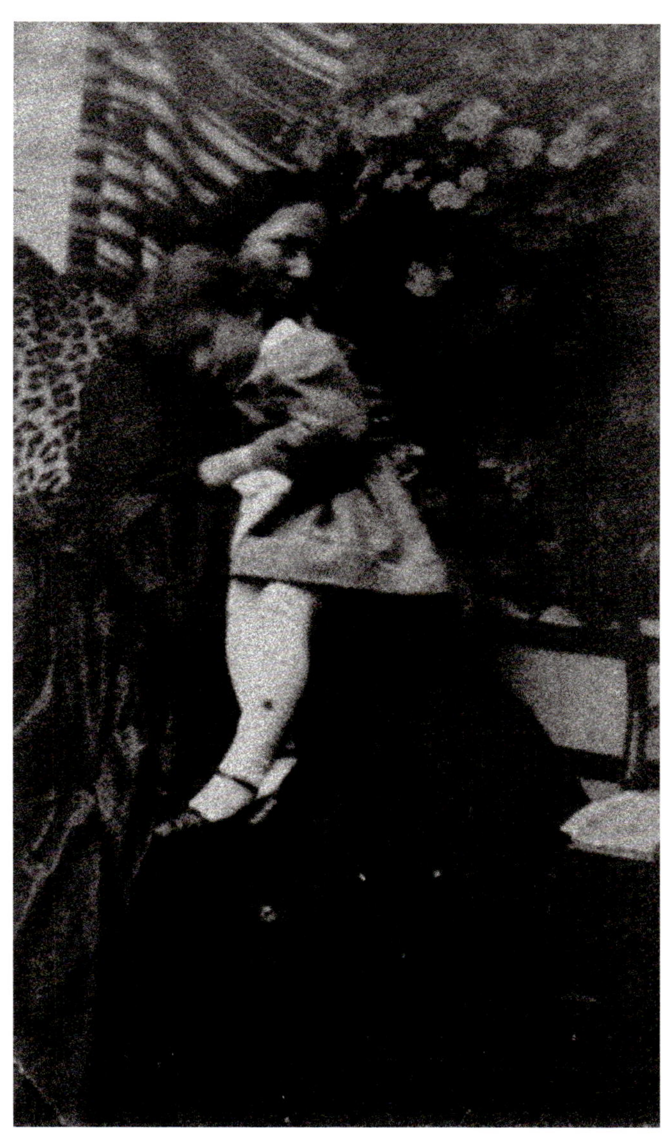

Unique extant Charles Lutwidge Dodgson photograph of Laura Wilson Taylor holding John Wycliffe (1863)

Characteristic of his organizational habits and determined ideas on how to do things "the right way," he engaged a carpenter to make shelves in a downstairs room for his archive boxes – to be precise, 132 of them. Each box was filled with paper (thus the "paper room") and each box was labeled with such titles as "Articles," "Events and Exhibitions," "Lewis Carroll Society Meetings," "Illustrators," and "Theatre." In some cases, the material spread over several boxes. "Articles" eventually took up seventeen boxes; "Theatre" needed eight. In some boxes, Edward stored original material: letters, manuscripts, and photographs. Each box is divided with file folders, labeled in pencil with registration numbers, and the contents of each box is part of the collection spreadsheet.

When, in 2000, Alice's great-grandchildren decided to sell the family collection and Christ Church Library could not raise the money to keep it, they contacted Edward and he sprang into action. He photocopied a "large mass of material" and made copious notes for posterity in his database. Then he got into the middle of things at the June 6, 2001, auction at Sotheby's. At the sale, he was the

Shelves for 132 archival boxes

winning bidder for Lot 134, the Black Sun Press *Alice* with illustrations by Marie Laurencin (1932), limited edition, number 263 of 790 copies. The hammer total for the entire auction was £1,783,00. Through a dealer, Edward later added another seven books from this sale to his collection.

In 2008, living amid a library that surpassed 15,000 Carroll items as well as other books and materials, Edward settled upon its disposition after his passing. After visits and exchanges with the custodians of Surrey History Centre, in Woking, England, he revised his will to donate his collection there, where it will join the Dodgson Family Collection (which it complements very well). Larger items will go to Guildford Museum. Any duplication will go to the Oxford Story Museum. "Thus the collection will remain in a national archive for perpetuity, and continue to be a source for serious scholars and researchers to use and interrogate," he has stated repeatedly. His nephews are seeing to his wishes.

Thirty-Five Letters

While it is difficult to single out just one or two transcendent categories within the Wakeling Collection, its thirty-five letters are an especially impressive distinguishing quality in a number of ways. The earliest dates from 1866 and the latest from 1897.

In his scholarly fashion, Edward had also long been transcribing letters and adding them to a database. He included all the published Dodgson letters, together with many yet to be published. The database has more than 5,940 entries, many of them "received" by Dodgson, and these mainly come from the Dodgson Family Archive. The database also includes all the business letters Dodgson wrote in his role as Curator of the Common Room at Christ Church between 1883 and 1892.

Edward Wakeling

In his non-Carroll correspondence database, Edward was especially proud of two letters he received relating to an appeal for help. A fourth-year art history student at Andrews University was writing a dissertation on Carroll's photography, and wrote to him. On November 29, 2004, Edward answered, providing a list of books that should help, offering to respond to specific questions, and noting, "It is very easy to misinterpret what the Victorians had in mind when they took photographs." On December 1, the student wrote back to thank him and provide some comments on her research and thinking. She signed the letter, "Best Wishes, Catherine Middleton." She later became the Duchess of Cambridge and later the Duchess of Wales. She completed her degree and titled her dissertation "Angels from Heaven: Lewis Carroll's Photographic Interpretation of Childhood."

MORE FRABJOUS COLLECTIONS & COLLECTORS

CRANDALL
MALCOLM
NUHN
SEWELL

ET AL.

One of the earliest bits of advice seasoned collectors and dealers in collectibles give to people on the upward trail to a collection is "Narrow your focus." Along with that goes the advice to pursue what really interests and pleases you. And then the reality check: Know what's possible to collect in terms of availability and your financial means. Many fine and comparatively smaller Lewis Carroll collections that are not in this book followed that advice – to the pleasure and satisfaction of their owners. Those in this chapter are among those who followed it to distinction. These relatively large collections possess world-class holdings dominated and distinguished by a passion for and focus on one aspect or two within the world of Carroll and his works: Disney *Alice* and ephemera, illustrated editions of the *Alice* books, advertisements and ephemera, Carroll art, art, art.

Even the specialist collections among Carroll collectors are not immune to the lures of a range of other Carroll items – books, arts and crafts, adaptations, and such – many acquired as gifts. What these collections are not, however, are collections of tier one antiquarian books from Carroll's lifetime. Some of these items are represented, but these collections are much more representative of Carroll in the popular culture and the world of Carrolliana today and in the 20th century.

The Crandall Collection

Imagine two adult Carroll collectors being introduced in 1991 by a mutual friend who worked at Disneyland. For Matt Crandall, Disneyland is sacred ground. When he was six years old and visiting Disneyland with his dad, the Alice character stepped out of the parade of characters on Main Street and shook his hand. That was it. He did not wash his hand again that day because he did not want to wash off Alice. Metaphorically, to this day, he has not washed his hand of Disney Alice.

Wendy Crandall had many childhood Disney experiences growing up in southern California. She liked *Alice* books, had a few dolls, and slowly built up a collection. She dates her collection back to 1971, when she was ten years old. What she especially liked about the book and Alice is that "anyone can be Alice. She talks back – and talks back to the Queen. I could really relate to that."

While they met in 1991 and stayed in touch, they didn't "connect" until 1996. Wendy was living in northern Virginia and a long-distance romance wasn't ideal; she presented Matt with an Alice in Wonderland which-road-to-take situation. In 1999, Matt moved to Virginia. We're all mad here was a given; when they married, "Our wedding vows included a line about building a life together – including our collection," Wendy states proudly.

Today and for much of their married life, they've lived in a house in Virginia near Washington, D.C., adorned with Carrolliana. In 2008, they held an open house for members of the Lewis Carroll Society of North America (LCSNA) to visit their collection in person. Then in April 2021 they shared their home and collection via video (which is currently available on the LCSNA YouTube channel): walls covered in Carroll objects, bookcases filled, a downstairs office and large Alice room crowded with amazing items. The love and joy the Crandalls have for Carroll-related objects shows. They do not hesitate to use the term "Carroll obsession." They are even known for wearing Carroll-related clothing – multiple outfits, in fact: shirts and blouses made from Carroll-character-themed fabrics, scarfs, dresses, earrings, other jewelry, buttons…

The "wedded collection" contains about four thousand items, more than 90 percent strictly Disney. But many more items have moved in and out of the collection over the years, as their "no more room" extended to selling duplicates and items that were no longer wanted (for example, pins) online and at toy conventions, Disney fairs, and even LCSNA meetings. As Matt repeats, "If you don't sell, you can't buy."

♥

Wendy and Matt Crandall at home and alongside an Alice poster for the Disneyland attraction (2024)

♥

Wendy's collecting interests extend well beyond books, and she relishes the opportunity to enumerate their general collection. "Name any object and I will tell you that we have it in Alice," she says. They have original posters, wallets, soaps, "mountains" of figurines, and "even a child's potty." And, of course, Disney.

The Crandalls estimate that more than 10,000-plus Carroll items have passed through their hands. One of the reasons is that around 2008 they decided to keep the items in their general collection that they prized for emotional or financial value reasons, but going forward to focus on Disney – and especially items associated with the 1951 Disney full-length cartoon *Alice in Wonderland* and earlier films.

WHY DISNEY?

Why Disney? Why Carroll? "Because we both grew up with Disney, as we both lived in southern California and visited Disneyland regularly," Matt says. And while Wendy loved the book growing up, both of them were heavily influenced by their experiences at Disneyland with Alice, "especially the dark ride" (a ride in a caterpillar-themed vehicle passing through specially lit scenes from the *Alice* films).

The 1951 Disney film became a touchstone for their collection because "it is an extension of the Disneyland experience. Since all those things at the park are based on the film, that is what we gravitated toward," Matt says – with Wendy close by his side. "While we had been focusing on strictly Disney since 1999, the decision to restrict the collection to the 1951 film release and before (and the odd item that was of special significance to us) was born out of necessity. Disney is a merchandise machine, and as Alice grew in popularity, the amount of merchandise grew

Original cel from the 1951 Disney film *Alice in Wonderland*, signed by Walt Disney on the mat frame

exponentially, so we decided to divest ourselves of all the new items and focus on vintage, for financial and sanity reasons."

It makes complete sense that one of the highlights of their collection is a cel from the 1951 movie, signed on the mat by Walt Disney. Another is the Disneyland attraction poster hanging in their home. They both saw it every time they went to Disneyland because it was on display to advertise the Alice dark ride. Theirs is one of the original hand-pulled silkscreen posters.

Kathryn Beaumont is associated with Disney's *Alice in Wonderland* – the young British actress ably provided

♥
Full set of Carroll-inspired figurines by Goebel (1951–1952)
♥

Alice's voice to the cartoon Alice of the film (and later voiced Wendy in the Disney film version of *Peter Pan*). She is an official Disney legend, and it can be said that the Crandalls collected her as well…as a dear friend. Matt met her first, in 1994 when a mutual friend introduced them at the Marc Davis Celebration of Animation at the Academy of Motion Picture Arts and Sciences. Over the years Kathy and Matt became friends, and when Wendy visited Matt in California in 1997, he introduced her to Kathy. After the move to Virginia, Matt and Wendy continued to visit Kathy on every trip to Los Angeles (including a few to Disneyland), and she visited them twice in Virginia – once for Wendy's fiftieth birthday, and again for the 2016 Geppi's Entertainment Museum exhibition of Alice items from the Crandall Collection.

A prize collecting adventure and acquisition occurred in fall 2011. Matt came across a very brief description of a piece of art that "piqued" his interest in an upcoming

David Hall watercolor (1939)

auction at a fine art auction house he was not familiar with. One lot was described as "David G. Hall Jr., Alice in Wonderland, 1939, watercolor on paper." There was no image. "So I emailed requesting images and a condition report," Matt explains. "They sent the image, and I recognized it from both a 1943 Disney book called *Surprise Package*, and also from a 1987 *Alice's Adventures in Wonderland* published by Disney, fully illustrated by David Hall (with a foreword by Brian Sibley). I kept the auction a secret for nearly two months." When the auction went live online, Matt sat at his computer with Wendy cheering him on. The lot was near the middle of the auction, so "we had time to wait, and we talked about limits, and had fun looking at what other people were buying. And then the lot comes up, and my absentee bid

♥

Mary Blair artworks, ca. 1950: *Alice Falling* (Wendy's favorite) and *Alice in the Tulgey Wood* (Matt's favorite)

♥

is the high bid. Two more people bid, then I bid again, and then a very long pause. My wife is screaming at the computer, 'Close it! Close it!' And...I WON!!! I couldn't believe my insane luck, and I'm sure my friends in Los Angeles could hear me screaming from here in D.C."

Another non-Disney highlight of the Crandall Collection is a complete set of Goebel figurines from Germany (ca. 1951–1952), which took Matt twenty-three years to complete.

A prized Disney-related collection within the Crandall Collection is the Mary Blair concept art they have acquired over the years. The renowned Disney animator and artist is credited for color styling on the Disney 1951 *Alice in Wonderland*, and her concept drawings are acknowledged as influential throughout the movie. The Crandalls consider acquiring her Alice paintings "a milestone in our collecting lives."

The Malcolm Collection

The Malcolm Collection dates back to an acquisition made more than fifty years ago. "After discovering *The Illustrators of Alice* book when I visited London in 1972," relates Andy Malcolm," I was amazed to discover that *Alice* had been illustrated by so many artists and illustrators, from Salvador Dali to Peter Blake and Mervyn Peake to Ralph Steadman." Purchase made. Since then, he's been all in. Nowadays, his wife, Robin, tells him that he's "compulsive and obsessive when it comes to Alice." He still loves illustrated editions.

Back home in Canada in the 1970s, Andy started to visit Toronto bookstores on Saturdays. He would inquire if they had any *Alice* books and was told at many shops that a collector from Toronto always got first dibs on any *Alice* book that came into their store. "I always wondered who this person was, and one Saturday, I waited in my favorite shop for this mysterious collector to show up,"

♥
Andy Malcom (front) and George A. Walker working in their Cheshire Cat Press studio
♥

Andy recalls. The person turned out to be Joseph Brabant, a prominent and internationally known collector focused exclusively on Lewis Carroll. "We became fast friends," says Andy, "and I was invited to his home to see his amazing collection. That's when I realized what it meant to be a serious collector. His dedication and passion for collecting was a great incentive for me." After Joe's passing, Andy was determined to continue in the tradition that he inspired.

In 1981, Joe, Bill Poole (printer and typesetter), and George Walker were the founding members of Cheshire Cat Press. They worked on publishing two new hand-printed editions of *Alice's Adventures in Wonderland* and *Through the Looking-Glass,* with original wood engravings by George Walker. In 1997, Joe's health deteriorated to the point where he could not complete the project. He chose Andy to write the introduction, making him the fourth member of Cheshire Cat Press.

That deep friendship came full circle when George and Andy revived Cheshire Cat Press in 2015. Since then, the fine press publisher of limited-edition books has focused on Carroll-related volumes. The first project in 2015 included illustrations by Harry Furniss for *Alice's Adventures in Wonderland* in a limited-edition folio. The press has published ten Lewis Carroll–related books as of 2024 and have four more in the works. Some of these publications are taken from Andy's collections of *Punch* cartoons, Guinness ads, magazine covers, advertisements, and comic books.

Pat Andrea illustration for *Through the Looking-Glass* (2015)

WHY CARROLL? WHY ILLUSTRATIONS?

While the Malcolm Collection – housed in a large rural farmhouse an hour's drive north of Toronto – contains objects relating to various aspects of Carrolliana, including translations, parodies, adaptations, spin-offs, ephemera, promotional materials, biographies and photographs, its focus is more than a thousand illustrated *Alices*.

Since the iconic John Tenniel illustrations, many "artists have approached the story with unique perspectives and styles, and I'm drawn to these visions," explains Andy. "Each illustrator contributes their style and influences on the book's overall atmosphere and visual

♥

Double page Ralph Steadman illustration to *Through the Looking-Glass* (1972)

♥

aesthetic." The fantastic world Carroll has created, "with its eccentric characters and nonsensical logic, makes it enjoyable for me. The dual-layered nature of his works has allowed me to appreciate them on different levels. Carroll's story allows for the interpretation of his eccentric characters and environments." Andy echoes what so many others have said: "Carroll's work is timeless, and the *Alice* books have achieved iconic status in popular culture, ensuring a built-in audience for any artistic interpretation. The story's enduring legacy and its timeless themes of curiosity and exploration continue to resonate with audiences of all ages, making it a subject of never-ending interest for artists around the world."

Andy still loves John Tenniel's work. Some years ago the question came up of what would be a super, super fiftieth birthday present. He received a first edition of *Through the Looking-Glass*. Talk about all in.

♥

Krill Chelyuskin's "Down the Rabbit Hole" (2012)

♥

Overleaf: Two-page spread from *Alice's Adventures in Guinnessland* (2021)

♥

Among Andy's favorite illustrators in the Malcom Collection are Kirill Chelushkin, Tove Jansson, Peter Blake, Harry Furniss, Kuniyoshi Kaneko, Pat Andrea, and Mervyn Peake, as well as some of the many Russian illustrators and editions he has collected. Like many major collectors in this volume and as a devotee of illustrations, his Salvador Dali edition of *Alice's Adventures in Wonderland* holds special pride of place. So does a signed Ralph Steadman *Alice*.

Steadman's style is uniquely his own, Andy says with appreciation. It's characterized by bold lines, chaotic compositions, dynamic energy, and exaggerated characters. Steadman is known for injecting a sense of subversion and satire into his work, often challenging conventional norms and authority. This distinctive approach adds a fresh and unconventional perspective to the classic tale of the *Alice* books.

Copies of this page may be obtained from Arthur Guinness, Son & Co. (Park Royal) Ltd., Advertising Dept., London, N.W.10

G.E.2183

76

'Tis the choice of the gourmet...

. . . I heard him declare,
" What matters the menu if Guinness be there?
Be it duck Bigarade, be it chicken Suprême,
It is Guinness we epicures really acclaim,
And oysters and lobsters and fish of the sea
Without it are sawdust and ashes to me.
But I really don't mind if you dish up a stone—
I would cheerfully banquet off Guinness alone."

I passed by his table, and marked with what care
He poured out the nectar, so foaming and fair,
And how fondly he gazed at the head, like thick cream,
And the velvety depths with their ruby-like gleam.
I saw with what fervour (but no undue haste)
He savoured in sips that delectable taste.
To see him so relish that Guinness, I thought it
An honour—though 'twas for myself I had bought it.

GUINNESS IS GOOD FOR YOU

Copies of this page may be obtained from Arthur Guinness, Son & Co. (Park Royal) Ltd., Advertising Dept., London, N.W.10 G.E.2178

77

Andy finds Russian illustrator Kirill Chelushkin rings a unique cultural viewpoint to his illustrations *of Alice's Adventures in Wonderland*. They often feature imaginative reinterpretations of familiar scenes and characters from the story. By putting his own creative spin on these elements, he offers readers a fresh perspective on the story while still honoring its classic roots.

Dali's illustrations for *Alice in Wonderland* very much appeal to Andy. They contain symbolic elements and hidden meanings that invite the reader to delve deeper into the subconscious realms of the mind. Dali's surrealistic, dreamlike, and fantastical imagery explores themes of identity, transformation, and the illogical nature of reality, adding a layer of psychological depth to the story.

MORE (THAN) CHESHIRE CAT

Since Cheshire Cat Press has been publishing Carroll-related books, Andy and George Walker have collaborated with many Carrollians to write introductions and share information and images from their collections. "In a funny way," Andy says, "I am collecting collectors."

As many of the collectors in this volume have expressed, Andy believes one of the great things about being a Carroll collector and enthusiast is the people you meet along the way. He recalls fondly meeting Edward Wakeling at a conference in Oxford in 1982, subsequently staying a few times with him in Herefordshire, and "always going on the hunt for Carroll books and building my collection in the bookstore Mecca of Hay-on-Wye." Edward also wrote introductions for three Cheshire Cat Press publications.

Carrollians, at least at first, are surprised to learn that their enthusiastic and outgoing fellow participant in the metaphorical Alice caucus races is legendary in the film industry as a sound editor and foley artist who has won many film awards, including an Emmy, and has credits on approximately seven hundred motion pictures. (A foley

Covering Alice, a Cheshire Cat Press book featuring appearances of Wonderland characters on a variety of magazine covers (2023)

artist is the one who creates sound and uses it creatively, so the sound effects are perceived as real.) That's Andy's work you can hear on *Barbie* (2023), *Dune* (2021), *Ford v Ferrari* (2019), *Blade Runner 2049* (2017), and Tim Burton's *Alice in Wonderland* (2009). In a brilliant career, only a Carrollian would say, as Andy does, that the experience working on the *Alice* film was "one of the highlights of my sound career."

His film *Sincerely Yours: A Film About Lewis Carroll* (2004) recreated Carroll's world and life. His documentary *There's Something About Alice: Alice's Adventures in*

Popular Culture (2022) was a decade in the making and included more than fifty interviews and collected thoughts from most of the collectors profiled in this book, and other scholars and collectors worldwide.

The Hirshon Collection

Another splendid Carroll collection heavily focused on illustrated editions of the *Alice* books belongs to Arnold Hirshon, current president of the Lewis Carroll Society of North America and the vice provost and Lindseth Family University Librarian Emeritus at Case Western Reserve University. An authority on the approximately 1,200 artists who have illustrated the *Alice* books, Arnold recently published a lengthy personal essay, "On Becoming a Curiouser and Curiouser Carrollian Collector" (*Alice in the World of Wonderlands*, Vol. 1, 2023) that we agreed covered his passion and collection more than a similar but much-reduced entry here would. His personal narrative is also a companion piece to his authoritative, scholarly book-length essay in the same volume, "Beyond Tenniel: The Evolution of Visual Representations of Wonderland by Illustrators of the English-Language Editions," which is extensively illustrated in color, with many images reproduced from copies in the Hirshon Collection.

The Richards Collection

London-based Mark and Catherine Richards are well-known Carrollian authorities and collectors through their publications and public presentations. Rather than being distinguished by an in-depth specialization and focus, their collection resembles the more comprehensive nature of the major collections profiled earlier in this volume. The Richards Collection contains Carroll-related printed matter and ephemera, including thirty-six photographs by Carroll plus six glass-plate negatives, early editions of

Carroll's books in variant bindings, thirty letters written by Carroll, more than three thousand postcards, theater programs and ephemera, extensive research materials, especially relating to Carroll's logic papers, an extensive collection of materials related to the events of the 1932 centenary celebrations of Carroll's birth, and many representations of illustrations and fine arts.

The Nuhn Collection

The impressive Nuhn Collection and its owner check a lot of boxes. The collection celebrated its fiftieth anniversary in 2024. Its 2,500 to 3,000 items live in their own room painted in a color called Alice Blue. Owner and collector Dayna Nuhn inherited the collecting gene from her parents, both collectors (though not of Carroll), and believes (as do many collectors in this volume) that you are born a collector and there is no cure. Dayna also shares the belief of most significant Carroll collectors that "although it sounds corny, the most valuable thing I have is the friendships I have made through collecting. Collectors help you find things you need, gift you with items, and have an incredible amount of knowledge to share."

What is especially impressive about Dayna and her collection is her focus. She is a role model for heeding the universal advice for collectors to narrow their focus and pursue what really interests them and can be achieved. "Dayna has developed an astonishing collection by focusing on 'flat things,'" says Carrollian Stephanie Lovett. "I would never have guessed, even though I like ephemera, what she would be able to find and interpret."

The first purchased item in the Nuhn Collection was not flat; it was a set of Beswick China figurines of characters from *Alice in Wonderland* purchased when Dayna was eighteen years old. But she learned quickly to zero in on her specialized area. "When I was in Oxford

Dayna Nuhn in her Alice room, 2024

for the 1998 Carroll Centenary Programme," she explains, "I saw and heard about all these amazing collections – of books. It was quite clear that I could never amass a collection to rival those. I knew I had to specialize if I ever wanted to create a significant collection. It was that same time that I learned about eBay, which opened a whole wide world to someone who lived in a small town in Canada near Toronto." She had a friend who collected Victorian ephemera, and her love of paper collectables rubbed off on Dayna, just in a different direction. Dayna decided to collect Carroll-related ephemera, starting with advertising and paper toys (card games and decks, paper dolls, toy theatres, etc.), then sheet music, and later valentines.

Known as the Flat Alice collector and authority on *Alice*-inspired advertising, she built a collection that includes about 350 magazine and newspaper ads, plus blotters, calendars, trade cards, booklets, cigarette cards, showroom materials (stand-ups), banners, and pamphlets that relate to advertising but aren't actual ads. The collection includes some 127 single songs and books of sheet music, about 45 valentines, more than 200 paper dolls, cut-out works, reference books, and parodies. There are also more than a hundred card games and card decks.

The remainder of the collection is filled out with books (at least 1,100). The Nuhn Collection includes copies of Carroll books (both editions of works and reference works about him and his art) and parodies, as well as tins, art, press kits, bookmarks, postcards, cookbooks, coloring books, greeting cards, figures, toys and games, china, Gerald King's (and others') stamps, some puzzles, book plates, and fabrics.

Dayna asks and answers the question of why anyone would collect Alice-inspired advertising in her introduction to *Alice's Adventures in Advertising* (Cheshire Cat Press, 2023). "I love seeing how creative people take Carroll's stories and characters and make something new and unique from them," she writes. "It is fascinating to see the original ways the *Alice* books can be linked to such a wide range of products, and also how multiple companies with quite different products can take an incident in the story, for example Alice's growing and shrinking, and adapt that specific concept to sell their particular goods or services. The same character or situation can be the source for many ads for quite different products." Dayna writes the column "Alice in Advertising-Land" for the Lewis Carroll Society of North America's *Knight Letter* (and is the editor of *The Snarkologist,* a journal dedicated to Carroll's *The Hunting of the Snark*).

She rightly points out that the *Alice* books have appeared in advertising for almost as long as the books have existed, and that many people who have not read the books nevertheless recognize and love Alice, Carroll's language, and the world of Wonderland – making them all attractive to advertisers. Alice "has been used to sell almost everything imaginable, both the expected and the

♥
Fender guitar ad (1975)
♥
Club Med ad (1993)
♥

unexpected products: from electric guitars to Ex-Lax, and from teapots to translators," Dayna says. She believes that when you look at a broad collection of ads spread out over decades, "they are windows that allow us glimpses into the past."

Dayna has some favorites in her advertising collection. She is "excited" by a rare set of Anchor Cotton trade cards, for example. The characters have spools of thread for bodies. (They are, indeed, advertisements for spools of thread.)

She especially likes cut-out and paper dolls. For years she coveted the rare Byron Sewell paper dolls, and despaired over never acquiring a set. Originally printed in an edition of thirty copies in 1979, Sewell encouraged the recipients to color and cut out the outfits because "what is the use of a paper doll if it isn't cut out and pretty?" After she met Byron, she wrote to ask if there

♥

Anchor Cottons advertising trade cards featuring *Alice* characters with spools of thread for bodies (ca. 1890)

♥

Sheet of paper dolls by Inga-Karin Eriksson (1993)

♥

Two outfits from Byron Sewell paper dolls (2nd ed. 1980)

♥

Dayna Nuhn Lozinski's wedding present from her husband

were any more copies. There were not, but "Byron managed to get one set back and he sent it to me. That was thrilling. They also were printed in a one-and-a-half page feature in the *Village Voice* newspaper in 1986, and collector Alice Berkey sent me a copy of that issue," says Dayna. "I could go on and on with stories about the kindness and generosity of collectors."

As in many collections, there are subcollections within the larger holdings. For the Nuhn Collection it is anything relating to the 1932 centenary celebrations of Carroll's birth, which, as Carrollians know, included a visit by Alice Hargreaves herself to New York. Dayna's 1932 collection consists of books, exhibit catalogs, programs, tickets, articles, news photos, postcards, and pamphlets. Collector Eldridge R. Johnson lent the original copy of the manuscript that he purchased from Alice in 1928 to a centennial exhibition at Columbia University, and subsequently commissioned a limited and privately printed edition that meticulously reproduced the manuscript for *Alice's Adventures Under Ground* that eventually appeared in 1936 in an edition of about fifty copies. One of those volumes holds a special pride of place in the Nuhn Collection. "My husband gave me a copy of this rare book as a wedding gift," Dayna says. "The book was a lovely gift by itself, but tucked into the pages was a reprint of an article, 'Auctioning Alice,' a photograph of Alice Liddell Hargreaves with her granddaughter, and a letter from Caryl Hargreaves to Eldridge Johnson."

The Sewell Collection

In the history of Lewis Carroll collections and collectors, Byron Sewell stands out as an original. He has been like a tornado with a smile blowing through the field, touching everything. For starters, he built not one but two major Carroll collections in his lifetime.

Byron is not only a noted Carroll collector but an illustrator, translator, bibliographer, parodist, and author – all with distinction. He's often been a speaker on things Carrollian, a connector of things Carrollian, and a prolific producer of things Carrollian.

Byron Sewell (ca. 2020)

His obsession with Carroll and *Alice* began as an adult. Byron studied studio art at the University of Texas at Austin, and had a fifty-year career involving facilities design all over the world. One of his earlier overseas assignments was a year-long engagement in London, beginning in 1971. As he likes to tell it, on a whim he bought a copy of *The Annotated Alice* to read on his long flight from Austin to London. By the time he landed, he was hooked for life. He had not read *Alice* before then, and has only a boyhood memory of the characters and story obtained from the 1951 Disney animated movie.

He returned from England with a "nice starter collection" of old *Alices,* and promptly hit the American antiquarian bookshops and beyond in search of early

♥
The Sewell-illustrated
The Hunting of the Snark (1974)
♥

American editions. Byron bought and bought, and cataloged and researched, while broadly collecting everything paper-related to Carroll – that means many editions of Carroll's works and works about them, boxes and boxes of ephemera, including programs and notices of theater performances, information about radio, TV, and movie collections, and a good assortment of translations of the *Alice* books. About ten years of hard research resulted in Byron becoming the absolute authority on early American *Alices*, and the eventual publication of a bibliography of those editions from 1880 to 1960, *Much of Muchness,* in a limited edition of seventeen copies (1992). It was privately reprinted in 2017, with two hundred covers printed in color.

At the same time that Byron was starting to collect copies and information on the early American editions of *Alice*, he also had the idea of picking up his drawing pen and illustrating *The Hunting of the Snark*. Then he decided the great Martin Gardner, whom he had never met, should write the introduction to his illustrated edition. Remarkably, that is what happened; the Catalpa Press, London, deluxe edition of *The Hunting of the Snark* appeared in 1974. Byron signed all 250 copies of the elaborate edition, with its pocket inside the back cover holding cards with sections of the crew members' faces, so they can be resorted. Byron's wit is evident in several other special effects in the handsome volume, such as the disappearance of the Baker, achieved by means of a transparent red sheet, and images that fold out for sixteen feet. His dedication to quality is everywhere present.

Within just a few years of starting his Carroll adventures, Byron had already created and acquired many sought-after collectible items. More were to come. As he says about himself in retrospect, "I have produced a rather large number of books, pamphlets, short stories, parodies, bibliographies, a few paintings, lots of illustrations, and various bits and pieces of ephemera, all on a Carrollian theme." Indeed, his contributions and his collections over the past six decades merit representation in this book on the outstanding Carroll collections and collectors. Every collector and collection here has been touched by Byron. His inclusion here is an exception only because there is no longer a Sewell Collection in private hands.

The story of the fate of the first collection is straightforward. As Byron has often said, when he was

♥

Sewell"s illustrated face cards from his *The Hunting of the Snark* (1974)

♥

♥
Byron and Victoria Sewell (2013)
♥

compiling *Much of Muchness* and acquiring all those books and ephemera, and creating all his wonderful art, his first wife, Susan, accused him of "loving the Carroll books more than I loved her." No doubt that's part of a not-simple story. But as a result, they went their separate ways, and in 1984, donated the Byron W. Sewell and Susan R. Sewell Collection of Lewis Carroll to the Humanities Research Center, now known as the Harry Ransom Center, at the University of Texas at Austin.

Happily, Byron later married Victoria. They have been together for more than forty years, and raised two children and a second Lewis Carroll collection. In name it is the Victoria J. Sewell Lewis Carroll Collection, in which Byron had play privileges. Its beginning dates to 1984. Byron is quite modest about his own ravenous collecting habits, and nobody had details of the breadth of the second collection that he and Vicki had amassed until 2015, when they put on an exhibition at the Huntington Museum of Art in West Virginia for the Alice 150 celebrations, complete with catalog. That catalog runs 717 pages and identifies and annotates more than 6,000 items in the collection.

Byron's intense work habits were on display across a wide audience of Carrollians. When Byron was in one of his prolific spurts (which seemed constant), fellow collector Alan Tannenbaum notes that he and wife Alison "would receive one of his (severely) limited editions of his latest brainstorm. Parodies were the mainstay, but humorous articles or cartoons based on current events were peppered throughout. At one point, it felt like we were receiving a one-page work from Byron every day!" Alan has file drawers dedicated to collecting Sewell; "In the first decade of our friendship, I received no less than one hundred original Sewells!"

Sewell illustration for the *Alitji in the Dreamtime*: "Looking up, she was startled to see the Wild Cat / Ngaya panyatja nyangu munu urulyaranu" (1975)

Byron Sewell's illustration of a coal miner as the White Rabbit (2012)

Vicki, who is from West Virginia, and Byron retired to Florida but had to leave behind about ninety boxes of Lewis Carroll books in a storage facility in West Virginia. When Byron and Vicki attended a meeting of the Lewis Carroll Society of North America at the University of Florida, Gainesville, in November 2022, Byron, then age eighty-one, announced quietly to his Carrollian friends and co-conspirators in many Carroll adventures that his memory was failing and he had difficulty speaking. His health has not improved. Among Vicki's stresses were those ninety boxes of books in storage and their eventual disposition. A year later, a novel plan was hatched. Vicki would keep the small number of items of significant commercial value and give the rest away for more or less the cost of shipping each random box. With the help of some fellow Carroll collectors and friends, un-birthday boxes were shipped to anyone who was willing to pay for a box, or two or three, and the rest were distributed

♥

The Sewell, Burstein, and Tannenbaum bibliography of Lewis Carroll in the comics (2013)

♥

on a first-come basis to children, schools, and enthusiasts. It was an admirable dissolution of the second great Sewell Collection. Now all sorts of Carroll books acquired lovingly by the Sewells are enjoying new homes across North America.

Byron's contributions will live for years to come. Among his many published works are *Alitji in the Dreamtime,* translation into Aboriginal Pitjantjatjara arranged and illustrated by Byron while working in Australia in 1975; a Korean translation, *Sun-hee's Adventures Under the Land of Morning Calm* in 1990; and even a dialect translation, *Alices Adventures in an Appalachian Wonderland* (2022). Byron and Vicki retold the story as a late 19th-century Appalachian folktale, and among Byron's Tenniel-inspired drawings is a Cottontail dressed as a miner in overalls checking "a big gold engineer's pocket watch." He coauthored *Pictures and Conversations: Carroll in the Comics* (2013), *An Annotated Bibliography of Lewis Carroll's Sylvie and Bruno Books* (2008), and numerous other works that will sit proudly on shelves and resonate in the minds of students, collectors, and fans of Lewis Carroll for generations.

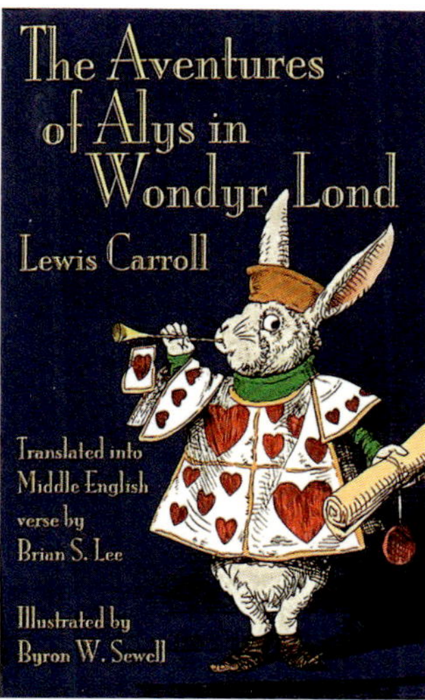

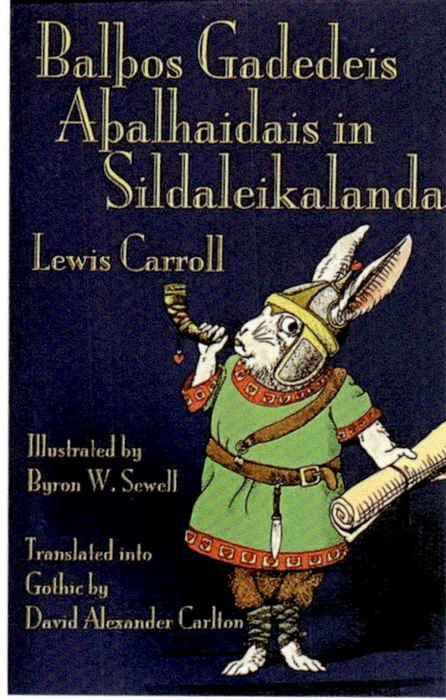

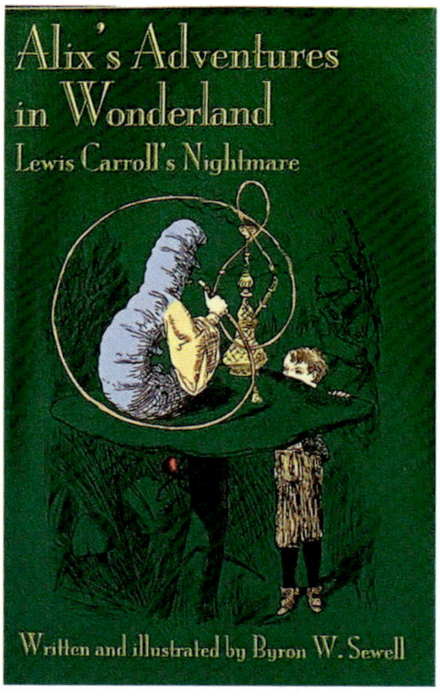

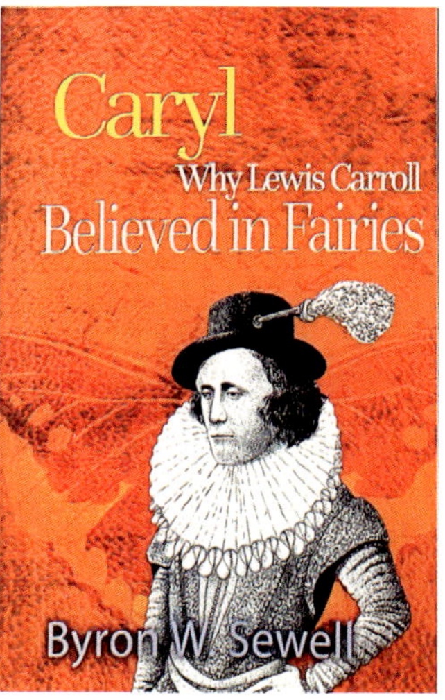

♥

Covers of Sewell-infused books published by Evertype, including their "Appalatchan Dialeck" edition translated and illustrated by the Sewells in 2012

♥

ACKNOWLEDGMENTS

Taking to heart the King's admonition in the trial scene of *Alice's Adventures in Wonderland* to "Begin at the beginning…and go on till you come to the end: then stop," how is it possible to begin these acknowledgments without thanking Charles Lutwidge Dodgson (Lewis Carroll) and Alice Pleasance Liddell first? Without them, this book never could have happened. Recalling Carroll's authorial intrusion in Chapter IX ("If you don't know what a Gryphon is, look at the picture"), I submit photos of Alice and a painting of Dodgson in the opening chapter, along with some observations on their apt connections to some of the themes in this volume.

I am pleased to recognize all the collectors in this book who opened up their collections to me and patiently answered my stream of questions…repeatedly. I thank them for supplying many illustrations and for fact-checking an early draft of the essay on their collection and sparing me from some embarrassing doggerel and "misprunts." Special thanks and gratitude go to Mark Burstein, Clare and August Imholtz, and Alan Tannenbaum for encouragement and for helping with essays on collections in addition to their own, and to Charlie Lovett for early and sustained care for this project.

To the publication committee of the Lewis Carroll Society of North America goes my warm appreciation for their support and encouragement, and to the Board of the Society, especially President Arnold Hirshon and Treasurer (and former president) Linda Cassady for promoting this as an LCSNA and Virginia publication.

My collaboration and the Lewis Carroll Society of North America's productive relationship with the University of Virginia Press dates to my first book with them in 1980! For this volume, we both recognize and appreciate the welcome support, advice, and enthusiasm of Mark Mones, Editor; Eric Brandt, Director; and Jason Coleman, Marketing and Sales Director.

Much thanks and much gratitude go to Susan Knopf at Scout Books & Media, who, with her extensive publishing experience and professionalism, shepherded the idea of this book to its printed and bound copies.

Regarding further acknowledgments and permissions, the Lewis Carroll Society of North America and I acknowledge the long and generous endorsement the Dodgson Estate has given us in helping to see our books on the life and works of Charles Lutwidge Dodgson received by the public. Permissions were sought and granted for all items I believe require such provision, and I believe that all other materials used and presented here are either out of copyright or, if not, were used within the "fair use" provisions.

INDEX

Page numbers in **bold** indicate photographs and illustrations.

Lewis Carroll Society of North America
2578 Broadway, #556
New York, NY 10025-8844

ISBN 978-0-930326-15-9 (hardcover)
ISBN 978-0-930326-19-7 (ebook)

Library of Congress Cataloging-in-Publication data available upon request.

First edition published in 2024

Book produced by Scout Books & Media Inc
Susan Knopf, President
Copyedited by Beth Adelman
Designed by Benjamin English

1 3 5 7 9 10 8 6 4 2

Manufactured in Canada.

www.lewiscarroll.org

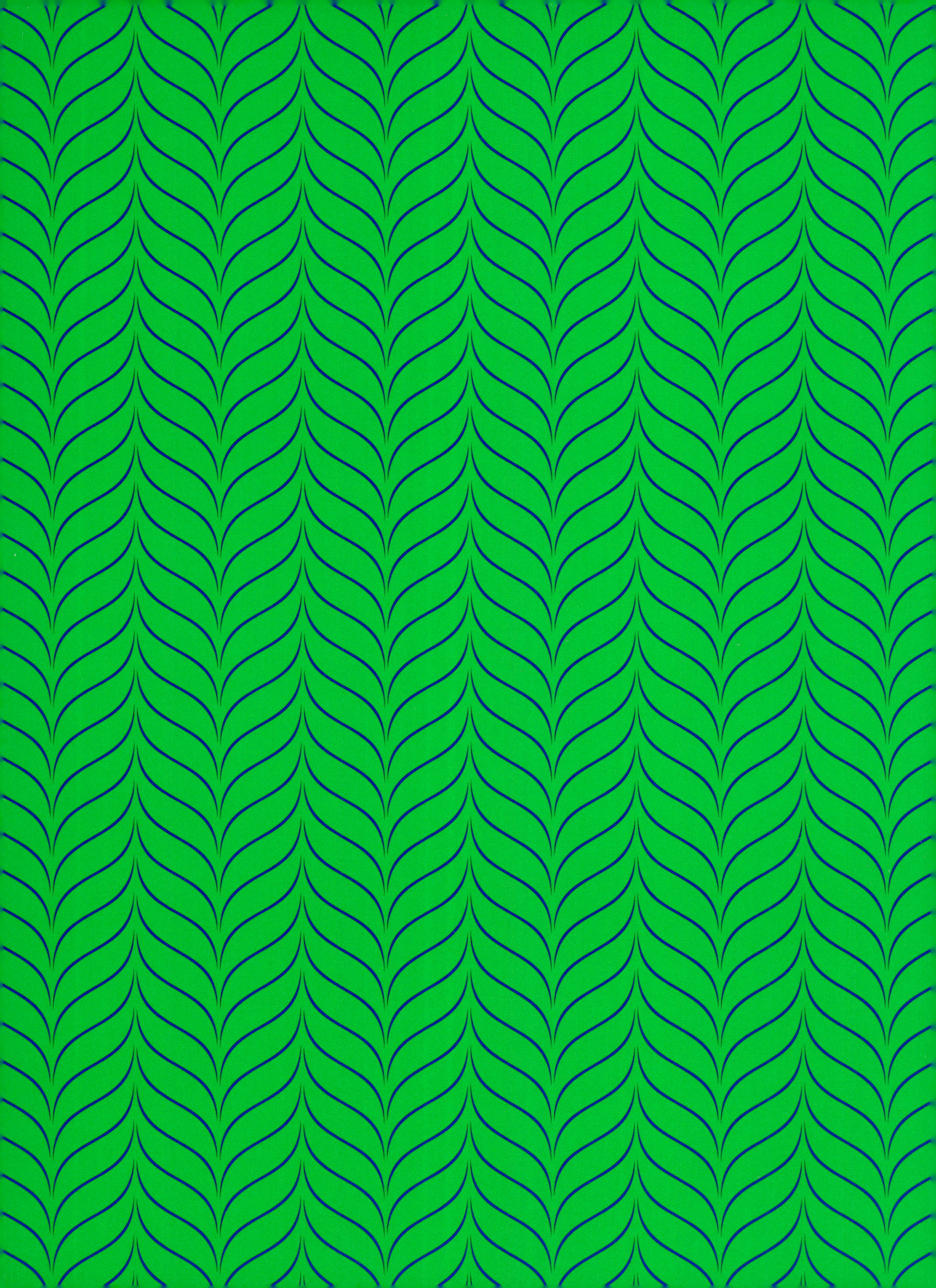